The Departure Platform

Also by Violet Powell

Autobiographical
Five Out of Six
Within the Family Circle

General
A Substantial Ghost
The Irish Cousins
A Compton-Burnett Compendium
Margaret, Countess of Jersey
Flora Annie Steel, Novelist of India
The Constant Novelist
The Album of Anthony Powell's Dance to the Music of Time (ed)
The Life of a Provincial Lady: A Study of E.M. Delafield and her Works
A Jane Austen Compendium

THE DEPARTURE PLATFORM

VIOLET POWELL

William Heinemann Ltd : London

Published in the United Kingdom in 1998 by
William Heinemann

1 3 5 7 9 10 8 6 4 2

First published in the United Kingdom in 1998 by William Heinemann
Random House UK Ltd
20 Vauxhall Bridge Road, London, SW1V 2SA

Random House Australia (Pty) Limited
20 Alfred Street, Milsons Point, Sydney, New South Wales 2061, Australia

Random House New Zealand Limited
18 Poland Road, Glenfield
Auckland 10, New Zealand

Random House South Africa (Pty) Limited
Endulini, 5a Jubilee Road, Parktown, 2193, South Africa

Random House UK Limited Reg. No. 954009

A CIP catalogue record for this book is available from the British Library

Papers used by Random House UK Limited are natural, recyclable products made from wood grown in sustainable forests. The manufacturing processes conform to the environmental regulations of the country of origin

Typeset by Deltatype Ltd, Birkenhead, Merseyside
Printed and bound in the United Kingdom by
Mackays of Chatham plc, Chatham, Kent

ISBN 0 434 00507 X

For John,
With love and memory of many travels

Contents

I
The Great Upheaval

To focus the circumstances of the Great Upheaval, it would be best to explain the Departure Platform from where this particular move took place. Immediately after our marriage, Anthony and I inhabited the two top floors of a house in Great Ormond Street. After two years in Bloomsbury we moved to 1 Chester Gate, an example of early nineteenth-century infilling. One of a pair of smallish houses – compared, that is, with the palaces of Chester Terrace – it stands in the piazzetta which leads from Albany Street into Regent's Park. This move was made in 1937. We were then without children and the house, with seven rooms if a basement sitting-room was counted, seemed positively spacious.

The Second World War drove us from our home like birds before a storm, but in the spring of 1943 we were able to perch at Dunstall Priory in Kent. This Regency villa sails like a ship over the Darenth Valley, which inspired Samuel Palmer to paint the most magical of his pictures. Dunstall Priory belonged to the poet Lord Dunsany, husband of my mother's sister. He loved the house even more deeply than his Irish castle and, at his own wish, was brought back to be buried in Shoreham churchyard.

After three years of departures there was something reassuring in settling in Dunstall, known from my childhood. It seemed the first step towards a return to normal life, instead of a nomadic existence. More than one generation of Dunsany's family had felt his own love for the white stuccoed house, lying under a steep cliff of beech trees, an emotion which had obviously left a feeling of home that transcended nationality. This became clear when Anthony invited a sequence of Allied officers to spend a day in Kent. These were associates with whom he worked in Military Liaison at the War Office, they being posted to the Military Attaché's office of their respective Governments in Exile. Without exception these visitors said that the landscape reminded them of France, Poland, Belgium, wherever, in fact, their homes had been on the continent of Europe.

Meanwhile, 1 Chester Gate stood empty, having miraculously escaped the bomb which had burnt its twin next door down to the ground floor. The escape was all the more miraculous because our total possessions – books, pictures, clothes – were still housed under this one roof. Slowly it became possible to arrange matters so that we could look forward not only to getting back into a home, but to having a place where Anthony, as a novelist, could hope to work.

Our attempts to regain our home were halted by attacks from flying bombs, V1s, whose main route passed immediately over the Darenth Valley and so over Dunstall Priory. To remove our son Tristram, aged four, from living under the regular track of these flying dragons with fiery tails was a top priority, but another period of impromptu moves was ended by a return to Chester Gate in time for Christmas 1944. It is true that V2s, whose speed was too fast to be signalled, were still being directed on London, but their advent, without warning, induced a fatalism which led almost to indifference.

As V2 rockets travelled faster than sound, they first manifested themselves by a trembling in the ground, followed, perceptibly later, by the noise of the explosion itself. There was, however, one morning when from my bed in Chester Gate I saw a glowing red worm wriggling down the grey sky of dawn. Then a shaking of the ground was followed by an explosion. I suddenly realised that I had seen the track of a V2 rocket, rather as an ornithologist might glimpse a rare bird.

Enemy attacks from the air were not the only cause for anxiety. Gabriel and Alick Dru were, at that time, installed in the top-floor bedroom over our heads. Gabriel was then expecting her second child and seemed to me to be cutting things rather fine. She had delayed returning to her West Country home in order to attend a party at the Cavendish Hotel arranged by Rosa Lewis, which Gabriel's brother, Auberon Herbert was to host. Undeterred by her condition, Gabriel danced round the floor with the Polish officers, friends of Auberon who was serving in the Polish Army. That night I quaked, though at a false alarm, when, lying below, I heard ominous footsteps overhead. Anthony and Alick Dru were then both majors in the Intelligence Corps at the War Office and the spare bed in the house was frequently occupied by Malcolm Muggeridge, yet another Intelligence Corps major. With rather laboured wit I found myself remarking that at moments I would gladly exchange three majors for one general (cook).

As he has recorded, Anthony was convinced that he would find the writing of even one novel impossible during a war. As a kind of insurance, to keep the creative engine turning over, he had started research on John Aubrey, the seventeenth-century antiquary. The resulting book, *John Aubrey and His Friends*, did not appear finally until 1950, when Anthony had already embarked on what was to be *A Question of Upbringing*, the first volume of *A Dance to the Music of Time.*

The opening of *A Question of Upbringing* finds the narrator, Nicholas Jenkins, happening on some road workmen clustered round a glowing brazier, on which snow is falling. This coincidence takes the narrator's memory back to classical times, and so to his school-days, largely dominated by the legends and language of the Ancient World. Some little time after the book had appeared, Anthony called to me to look out of the window of 1 Chester Gate. In the road outside, a hole had been dug and the workmen had lighted a brazier beside it. Deliberate snowflakes were falling, hissing as they hit the brazier. Prevision of something that may well happen is a gift belonging to the craft of novel writing, and the snow falling on the brazier could be called a classical example of this insight.

The death of the widower of Anthony's aunt, Violet Gabrielle Inglis, with whom I shared not only a Christian name but the initials V. G., made possible a move to larger premises and, in fact, to the country. Number 1 Chester Gate, which had once seemed so spacious, appeared to be getting ever smaller. There was a top bedroom shared by Tristram, now aged eleven, and John, five years old, but their only nursery doubled as a spare room for visitors such as Antonia and Felicia (nieces), Thomas (nephew) and Julia (sister). Anthony worked in the dining-room, at the mercy of the telephone and any caller.

Six years of war had battered the east side of Regent's Park, rebuilding having been delayed by a sensational fire at the end of Cambridge Terrace, which backed on to our house. This took place in the great freeze-up of 1947, but even an inferno next door did not generate enough heat to melt our frozen pipes. There had been a rumour that the caretaker, whose brazier was thought to be responsible, might have perished in the conflagration. 'How will they test the ashes?' enquired Toby Tennant, the ghoulish small son of the Glenconners, our neighbours.

Albany Street, as a shopping village, had, however, retained its pre-war variety, a butcher, a baker and, if an antique dealer could be included, a candlestick seller, if not maker. There was also a fishmonger, and a Welsh dairy man, who created the Anthony Powells as honorary kin of the Powells of Nanteos, Cardigan. I appreciated thus being linked with a family who owned the reputed Holy Grail, a wooden cup used locally to cure diseased cattle. Finally, when my protests that Anthony's Powells came from the Welsh border failed to shake Mr Edwards's conviction, I let the matter drop and even simulated an interest in the funeral of the Nanteos gamekeeper. The least salubrious shop-front in Albany Street belonged to a tailor, through whose begrimed windows could be read a notice boldly proclaiming 'Soonest with the latest'.

Nothing could have been more of a contrast than the shop that sold wools, which was presided over by a young girl of extreme blonde prettiness. There was a rumour afloat in Albany Street that she ran the shop as therapy for a nervous condition. Whatever the truth there was a surprise when Tristram, John and I visited her on an afternoon when the Upheaval was coming closer. I have long forgotten what purchase I wished to make, but in the course of conversation the shopkeeper mentioned that she knew our local clergyman, the Reverend W. V. C. Rose, Vicar of Christ Church, Albany Street. Mr Rose had not only christened John, but had been recruited by Anthony to arrange George Orwell's funeral. He had shown no discomposure at the variety of the congregation of mourners, some obviously distrustful of organised religion.

We were, however, startled to learn that Mr Rose and the blonde young lady belonged to a Society whose object was the study of the science of palmistry. She was immediately required to put theory into practice. Six rather grubby palms were laid before her on the counter among the balls of brightly coloured wool. She responded gamely to this challenge. For the boys she made the reasonable deduction that the younger was anxious to keep up with the doings of the elder. Then she looked at my hand and her reading had a surprising relevance to the prospect immediately before me.

The pattern of my life, I was told, was shortly going to change completely, not only in circumstances but in occupation. A new interest would develop, which might for a while run beside other interests, but would then outstrip them. Whether or not this girl ran her shop to soothe her nerves, I can only say that as a prophetess she scored a bull's-eye. In fact, she foresaw my future with far more clarity than I interpreted her message.

Moving to the country had seemed to me an opportunity to become a gardener, even a passionate horticulturalist. I had never before been more than a mustard and cress grower, nor had I had the prospect of a garden in which I could plant what I wished. I certainly did not foresee that the prophecy handed out from the Albany Street wool shop would be fulfilled not with a spade but at a typewriter.

It was not only our house that we were leaving. There was a very active social life in Park Square among contemporaries of both John and Tristram. Here there were swings and a sandpit for the smaller fry, whose mothers supplied them with basting spoons as spades. These were regularly lost and must have provided a metal foundation. There was a fascination for me in realising that a beautiful little girl with flowing pale-gold hair was a daughter of one of the six Meyrick sisters. Their mother had run the 43 Night-club in Jermyn Street. After her death the daughters, whom I had met in the 1930s, continued to run various night-clubs and bottle parties. Their behaviour was impeccably well-brought-up, and they treated the rather louche waiters as family retainers.

The brightest hair, however, belonged to the infant Jane Asher, its Pre-Raphaelite intensity emphasised by butcher-blue rompers. John's schoolmate, Bill Collins, had two elder sisters who could sometimes be seen lugging him towards the Francis Holland. Joan and Jackie Collins hardly need introduction, and their early charm is preserved in the group photographs of the Francis Holland School. When Joan Collins first crossed my view in Park Square, the glance of her eyes was such that I remarked, 'The girl who has just passed would get off with man, woman or child.'

The walk, in summer, across Regent's Park to the Francis Holland School was made interesting by the broadcast rehearsals from the Open Air Theatre, filling the air with exciting speeches – 'All Kent has yielded. Nothing there holds out but Dover Castle.' This was an early and painless introduction to Shakespeare for both Tristram and John. When the lake was reached there would be a second view of the heron who had already been seen flying across the park, punctually on his way to a morning's fishing. The heron sat on one of the posts that hindered unauthorised landings, creating a 'heron-priested shore' such as Dylan Thomas wrote about.

That summer was full of the sort of sunshine one would like to buy by the yard. This shone most brightly over Paris, where we went for a week to brace ourselves before the turmoil of moving. At that date Nancy Mitford was still living in her house in rue Monsieur. Her big sitting-room was, she said, like a lantern, its long windows looking out on to the courtyard in front and a secluded garden of pebbles at the back. Here Nancy sunbathed, only overlooked by one window, that of a bathroom of which she hoped the glass was opaque.

With one of Nancy's luncheon guests, the Marquis de Lestryac, we strolled through the Quartier St Germain. He enlivened the quiet streets by accounts of the dramas that had taken place in the big houses crouching behind their *porte-cochères*. Halting at a particularly imposing archway, Monsieur de Lestryac told me that the mansion behind it had been the scene of 'the famous *mariage blanc*', without, alas, giving the names of the frustrated partners.

At that moment the British allowance for foreign travel was twenty-five pounds, and Nancy complained that many of her friends regarded her as a bureau de change. She was, however, endearingly hospitable to Anthony and me. Her friendliness went so far as to come out to dinner with us.

This was a compliment, as she was believed to be loth to leave 7 rue Monsieur in the evening, for fear of missing one of Gaston Palewski's all too infrequent telephone calls.

On this evening we paused for a drink at the Deux Magots. It was there that one of the dubious art students, ever on the prowl with a sketch-book in search of gullible tourists, paused at our table. He accepted a rebuff in reasonably good part and, as he moved on, he patted the top of Nancy's curly head, almost a feature of her character. For a moment, deprived of sophistication, Nancy ducked down from the patting hand, squeaking, 'Oh, do go away.' This prosaically English lady's way of handling the situation sent the itinerant artist off in fits of laughter.

The most imposing of the mansions of Belgrave Square might be said to be the Spanish Embassy, which stands on the south-west corner. For as long as I can remember on the island outside the embassy's gates there has been stationed a barrow selling flowers, or rather a barrow with flowers for sale, speculation having frequently suggested that this might be an unusually beautiful form of surveillance. On the night that a ball was given for Caroline Child Villiers, daughter of my cousin Grandy Jersey, the flower barrow may not have done much business among the ball-going traffic, but its fragrance undoubtedly added a flourish to the warm June night. Sparkling the night was, particularly on the heads of the host's wife and his two sisters. For them, three tiaras had been extracted from Child's Bank, founded by an ancestor. I do not remember that Princess Margaret, then unmarried, wore a tiara, nor did Elizabeth Taylor, recently married – her second nuptials – to Michael Wilding. I was dancing with Harry d'Avigdor-Goldsmid, husband of Rosemary Nicholl, one of my oldest friends, when he suddenly asked me to stand by for a moment. I had hardly had time to take in the pause when he returned. Elizabeth Taylor had been brought to dinner at his home, Somerhill, and he had seized the opportunity to whirl her once round the floor. In the light of subsequent developments it is worth noting that Harry reported, sadly, that Miss Taylor was too much in love with Michael Wilding for any impression to be made on her.

William Heinemann had published *A Question of Upbringing* (1951) and *A Buyer's Market* (1952), and these might be called the launching pad from which *A Dance to the Music of Time* took off. At the garden party Heinemann gave to celebrate the opening of the newly built Windmill Press, in the coppices of Kingswood, Surrey, Anthony naturally had a number of friends among the management. Somerset Maugham – perhaps, figuratively, the tallest feather in Heinemann's cap – gave a speech declaring the buildings open, celebrating his relationship with a firm that had enabled him to keep the wolf from the door, while on their own behalf erecting this handsome edifice. Tea was then served, and a photographer circulated among the tables. There were a number of literary and stage celebrities among the guests, but obviously in the mind of Emlyn Williams there was no doubt as to who was the most worthy to be photographed. As it happened, the young lady from Heinemann in charge of the photographer was acquainted with Anthony in the way of business. She urged the camera man to our table, crying, 'Mr Powell, we must photograph you.' Meanwhile Emlyn Williams, who had risen to his feet, stood with a hand on his hip and a glare in his eye that would have done credit to his performance in *Richard III*.

By 1952 Osbert Lancaster, in his cartoons, had built up a cast of principals and bit players which had become as familiar to his readers as their own families. Maudie Littlehampton, Canon Fontwater and hatchet-nosed dowagers were sometimes joined by boy scouts and choristers, whose cherub faces usually contained a hint of moral turpitude. On the evening of a Royal Academy soirée, for which evening dress with decorations was decreed, Karen and Osbert Lancaster dined with us. Dinner was interrupted by the arrival of the curate from St Mary Magdalene, Munster Square, where I habitually worshipped. The curate, in shorts and a beret, had brought with him his troop of chorister boy scouts. They had come to collect the jam jars I had hoarded and when Anthony, bemedalled, and I in a hooped evening gown carried these up from the basement, Osbert had difficulty in believing that the tableau had not been staged for his benefit.

During our first years at Chester Gate Lord Gerald Wellesley was living opposite in a small house which was another example of infilling. The house owned a pleasant strip of garden, and he had placed a bust of John Nash to preside over the garden aspect, more as a titular deity than as the responsible architect. He was fond of quoting Gibbon – 'I sighed as a lover, but obeyed as a son' – when explaining that he had wanted to make architecture his career, but had followed his parents' wish that he should enter diplomacy. By 1937, when we moved into Chester Gate, he had managed to return to his first choice of profession.

Purists made unkind jokes about Nash's standard of workmanship, contrasting Augustus finding Rome brick and leaving it marble, with Nash finding London stone and leaving it stucco. Even if not built by Nash, Wellesley's house, 3 Chester Terrace, was in a permanent state of flaking, to such an extent that visitors looking across from our drawing-room asked if the house opposite had not been deserted for years. It had an inviting doorstep on which old men were apt to take a seat, to rest from a walk in the park. No dog failed to lift its leg against the railings, and it seemed that no child went past without giving a runaway ring.

It was only after World War Two that we became friends with Gerry, who had by that time become the Seventh Duke of Wellington, his nephew having been killed in Italy. My great-great-aunt, Kitty Pakenham, had been married, rather unhappily, to the First Duke of Wellington and Gerry cherished this connection as he did many other aspects of his dazzling ancestor. Apsley House and Stratfield Saye had both suffered from a lack of interest on the part of the two previous owners, but even on our 1952 visit to Stratfield Saye Gerry had taken matters in hand.

One of the First Duke of Wellington's domestic arrangements had been to install a number of water closets *en suite* and sometimes in corners of the principal bedrooms. In the years when Stratfield Saye was mostly uninhabited, a witchlike housekeeper and her black familiar, a cat called Smut, would, in theory, patrol the house. According to Gerry, this weird couple were unable to prevent all the pipes in the Duke's water closets from freezing, with consequent devastating bursts. The other memorial to the First Duke's domestic tastes, perhaps an exercise in therapy, were the prints which he had, with his own hands, pasted on to walls in the long gallery and in rooms upstairs.

Our later visits were, usually, to attend the Annual

General Meeting of the Jane Austen Society, but in 1952 the addiction for Jane Austen which I shared with Gerry had barely been discovered, and the chief diversion was a luncheon party at which the Duke of Alba with his daughter and son-in-law were guests. 'Alba's made his son-in-law a duke,' said Gerry. Having inherited a Spanish dukedom himself, he felt an interest in the subject, though he added, rather gloomily, that dukes were two a penny in Spain.

Later in the week a party from the National Arts Collections Fund were expected. In preparation for this visit we were led to inspect the Wellington state coach. Ignoring the cloud of moths that flew out of the elegant interior when he opened the door, Gerry explained that he hoped the coach would form part of a procession at the approaching coronation. This the coach did, though some other ducal owners proved recalcitrant. As we drove away on Monday morning I noticed a man standing before an easel, paintbrush in hand. Looking back to see what aspect of Stratfield Saye was being recorded, I found that in preparation for the cultural visitors the supposed artist was simply engaged in painting the word GENTLEMEN.

The Upheaval was drawing ominously near, but we had one last remission in the form of a Saturday to Monday with Rosemary and Harry Goldsmid at Somerhill. Breezes blew from across the northern aspect and the range of hills that separated the Wey from the Thames estuary, but the tennis court was ingeniously sheltered, sunk and surrounded by high banks. Hospitality at Somerhill was so lavish that stiff sets of tennis were a necessity between meals. On this visit Hugh Casson, who later became a knight and President of the Royal Academy, did a memorial sketch of the dining-room when the Sunday luncheon party had left the table, but the chairs and the table itself were still in disarray. Devoid of human figures the sketch wittily caught the moment when the company had, as it were, moved off-stage, but had left behind an afterglow of good cheer.

When the 'For Sale' sign went up on our balcony, some of the passers-by on their regular route to the park were kind enough to express regret, but I must admit that it was not so much at losing the Powells as at the prospect of losing Albert. This was our reigning cat, a tabby with a white waistcoat, who had the rather unusual feature of being attractive to dogs and liking them himself. His predecessor, Smoke, had only reigned briefly, being of a blue-grey colour indistinguishable at night. His fate was the same as Jude, the cat of Anthony's parents, who had been run over crossing from their house in Clarence Terrace on the opposite side of the park. A kind traffic policeman brought us Smoke's collar and, even more kindly, supplied a kitten, Albert, as a replacement.

Albert's favourite seat was on the dining-room window-sill, from whence he exchanged courtesies with his admirers. The most splendid of these was an Alsatian, who refused to pass the house until he had been assured of Albert's presence. Albert had been named after a wartime colleague of Anthony's, an assistant Belgian military attaché called Albert Lechat. We wrongly assumed that he was safely back in Belgium, but he suddenly reappeared in London to attend the Requiem for the ambassador under whom he had served. He asked if he could borrow the Sam Browne belt which Anthony's father had passed on to his son and which had been through at least two wars. We gave Lechat luncheon and found ourselves referring to Albert as 'Pussy' throughout the meal.

It was obvious that in our country home we would require a motor car, but the search was difficult. New cars were dreams at the end of a long waiting list. Even the strangest second-hand models had to be chased like shy animals. Some people managed to acquire London taxis, which had passed the date when they could be licensed to travel the streets of the metropolis. Anthony rather leaned towards a taxi, but I protested that I did not wish to become known in a new neighbourhood as a female cabbie.

Finally we bought an old Humber, even more ancient than the model which Colonel Powell had cherished since before World War Two. The bonnet did not present a too outmoded appearance, but the rear view, solid except for a tiny glass panel, looked only too like a taxi serving a village community far behind the times. This ponderous vehicle did inspire a certain awe among drivers coming from the opposite direction, but the local car auction, appropriately situated at Cannard's Grave, showed little enthusiasm when we finally put the Humber in for sale. We retained a floor mat whose Picassoesque picture of a horse suggested it belonged to carriage days. The days of the booming market for antique cars had yet to come.

In retrospect, it seems hard to believe that this summer of 1952 was blighted by a war scare. The consequence was that there appeared to be only one prospective buyer for any house in a desirable part of London. This solitary house hunter was accompanied by a dominating mother.

The latter's behaviour combined deprecating the house her daughter was inspecting with deploring the habits of owners who could live in such a shack. This technique was practised not only at Chester Gate, but at Victoria Grove, Kensington, and in Carlisle Square, Chelsea, where the would-be seller was reduced to tears.

An advance party, Anthony with Albert, wailing in a basket, and most of the furniture, left. I spent a last night alone in the house that I had often wished to be engraved on my tombstone because I felt its inconvenience would be the direct cause of my death. It had, on the other hand, seen what could be called the birth of the first two volumes of *A Dance to the Music of Time*. There had been bad moments when dry rot, in festoons worthy of Arthur Rackham, decorated the front hall and access was by the basement only, but the wave of scent from flowering trees and shrubs that rolled over one on turning into the park from Albany Street on a spring evening made the idea of living anywhere else unbearable. On this last night in Chester Gate I had little time for nostalgia. From all around, the night was rent by cats keening the loss of Albert until with the summer dawn I rose to take my departure to a new life.

II

'To arrive is to die a little' – Anthony Powell, *From A View to a Death*

A corollary of moving house is the emergence of old unhappy far-off things from long-forgotten cupboards, boxes of broken china to be riveted should the millennium arrive, presents of intense hideousness, but preserved from superstitious sentimentality. These are the last objects to be piled on to the last van, and consequently the first to be unloaded. We had left a house that was bursting at the seams, but the new home was to be filled only too quickly. The vagaries of a war scare meant that the metal pins for bookshelves were diverted to rearmament, and while wooden slats were awaited books grew whiskers on the stone floor of the basement.

Having written his early books at three different addresses in Bloomsbury, before moving to Regent's Park, Anthony had now to establish a new literary *querencia*. The view from The Chantry, wooded hills with glimpses of the lake at the bottom of the valley, at first seemed to him inimical to creative literature, and he chose to write in a room which looked simply into a yew tree. The book which had been, as it were, carried on from London to Somerset was *The Acceptance World.* It begins with a prophecy of a love affair, and ends with the ominous prospect of a break-up between the lovers. The first stitch of this pattern had been sewn in the opening chapters of what it is simplest to call *Dance*, and threads of the same romance would suddenly glitter in all but one of the later volumes.

Upheavals seldom come singly. Our move coincided with a professional change for Anthony. He left the *TLS*, where he had edited fiction, and became Literary Editor of *Punch*, whose editor Malcolm Muggeridge had recently become. Alan Pryce-Jones, Editor of the *TLS*, remained a friend, nevertheless, and came to Chantry in the spring of 1953, shortly after he had lost his most delightful wife, Poppy.

One of the first problems of estate management that came our way when we had moved in was dealing with the luxuriant growth of hay in the paddock opposite the front door. A local eccentric, who owned a tractor, was persuaded to cut the hay and, with assistance from Anthony, built a small haystack. This had become valuable at the end of the winter, when parents of pony club members were seeking fodder. It seemed easier to bring the ponies to the hay than vice versa and to allow John to ride one of these four-legged lodgers I had borrowed a saddle and bridle. This lay on the floor of the kitchen, which had not yet been modernised from the Mass Centre it had previously been. Alan must have been impressed with the display of horse tack for, soon after his visit, he sent me for review a book on Classical Equitation. Confident that I should not be asked to give a demonstration, I reviewed it and so started on the fulfilment of the prophecy made by the fortune teller of Albany Street.

Towards the end of Anthony's time at the *TLS*, he had reviewed *The Skin* (*La Pelle*) by Curzio Malaparte. The novel is concerned with the American forces in Naples at the end of World War Two. Malaparte cheerfully dedicated the book to his commanding officer USA and the rest of the brave soldiers with whom he had served, 'who had died in vain for Freedom'. I mention, in passing, that I happened to be reading this book in a restaurant car when the distinguished gentleman opposite enquired if it was a treatise on skin diseases. By a wild feat of memory I realised that he had taken the chair at a recent AGM and Wine Tasting of what was then the International Exhibition Co-operative Wine Society. I knew him to have been in the medical profession and, for reasons I shall explain, my denial was made in guarded terms.

The Skin might be called a study in the horrors of Liberation: Naples swarming with foreign troops, children sold to the French African *goums*, American negroes enjoying the golden 'wigs' which, worn under skirts, gave an illusion of a natural blonde. Gifts from the Liberators were lavish, but undoubtedly the most gigantic was the tank, which a besotted GI parked with a flourish outside the home of his loved one. The tank was swiftly driven into a neighbouring courtyard and in a few hours an oil stain on the earth was the only trace of this sumptuous, if inadvertent, gift from the United States Army.

Our first autumn at Chantry coincided with Tristram's last term at Sandroyd School, which had been evacuated to Rushmore House, Tollard Royal during the Second World War, and had remained in its wartime home. The situation of Rushmore, on the downs immediately outside Shaftesbury, is wonderfully romantic. It has still a lingering aura of its nineteenth-century owner, General Pitt-Rivers, who is even now respected for his advanced practices in applied archaeology. To parents, the noble avenues and sweeps of downland were among the assets of the school. Space for playing fields was unlimited and riders were immune from the danger of tarmac roads. Only the more sceptical parents wondered if their materialistically minded children might not have preferred an easier access to such urban delights as Woolworths.

The Grosvenor Hotel at Shaftesbury reaped a rich harvest from Sandroyd parents. On the last occasion that we gave Tristram luncheon in this hotel the chances of an army exercise had stationed two tanks in the town square. This gave an extra and welcome interest to a meal, which was usually only enlivened by contemplating the vast sideboard depicting the battle of Chevy Chase carved in high relief and stretching along an entire wall of the dining-room. Recollecting the incident in Malaparte's novel, I asked Anthony if he thought that any of the soldiers clustered in the foggy square would give a tank to his girl-friend that night. Tristram picked up the allusion, remarking, 'That comes in *The Skin*, doesn't it?' As he had obviously read at least some of the more extreme passages in the book, Tristram's parents could only feel he must have made a giant stride in sophistication.

The first Christmas in the new home set two patterns, which persisted for a number of years. Camilla and Christopher Sykes were living temporarily in a village beyond Stourhead. Consequently we were on their route to

Midnight Mass at Downside. Together with their son Mark, and any other guests, they came to call each Christmas Eve, decorous behaviour that was somewhat out of character in the case of Mark. Not herself a Roman Catholic, Camilla, always top in looks wherever she might be, could never quite decide what line to take. Sometimes she joined her husband and son in the church. Sometimes she sat in the motor car outside, armed with crosswords and describing herself as a Protestant chauffeur.

On Christmas Day a tradition began that my sister Julia, Robin Mount (her husband) and their children, Ferdie and Francie, should come to luncheon. The electric stove was adept at creating original crises on the morning of the festival. Few things are less festive than the voice from the Electricity Authority reciting the additional rates payable for repairs at the holiday season, but luncheon was always rescued and presented. Afterwards, a walk down the lane between Chantry and Mells was taken. On one occasion Anthony was disgusted by finding that a wreck of a perambulator had been discarded in a hedgerow. He struck a number of matches in an attempt to burn this blot on the countryside, which I suggested would have been more appropriate on 28 December, Feast of the Holy Innocents. We all agreed, however, that in a diary 'Set fire to pram' would be an original entry for Christmas Day.

Tristram's first half at Eton loomed at the end of the Christmas holidays, while John was changing to a school in Frome. There had been various panics about polio before we left London and I was paid out for my reluctance to risk the boys at swimming baths when it became clear that Tristram would need to reach a higher aquatic standard to pass a test at Eton for going on the Thames. The lack meant that we spent the early weeks of 1953 driving into Bath, where a gaunt man who looked like a dragon shouted instruction to Tristram, who paddled below. The public swimming bath bore no resemblance to 'the warm Bath' which plays such a key role in the happy ending of Jane Austen's *Persuasion*.

Jane Austen, as it happened, had had an influence on the house at Eton to which Tristram went. Faced with a list of those who might be expected to be housemasters when Tristram's age group went to the school, Anthony remembered that Francis Cruso had declaimed a passage from Jane Austen at Speeches, part of the Fourth of June Celebrations. This choice was made in the early summer of 1940, Tristram a bundle in a carry-cot and the future murky, not to say opaque, but the choice itself could not have been happier; Francis was not only a sympathetic and congenial housemaster to both Tristram and John, but remained a friend of their parents. Mothers notoriously worry housemasters about the progress of their children. I think I am possibly unique in having asked Francis to correct *my* grammar rather than that of my son. He was an expert on the novels of Ivy Compton Burnett, contributing a wonderfully witty account of a Compton Burnett Christmas to *Punch*, and he obligingly corrected the proofs of *A Compton Burnett Compendium*, my contribution to studies of Dame Ivy's works.

Until I left London, auction sales had mostly found me among the sellers; indeed, I once sold a kitchen clock that had long ceased to tick and a carpet cleaner which in demonological fashion produced noise rather than action for the princely sum of three pounds. I have always appreciated Lewis Carroll's argument that it is better to have a clock that never goes, which is indisputably right twice in twenty-four hours, rather than one which goes but, being ten minutes fast, is never right. Even Lewis Carroll would, I think, have found it difficult to produce an extenuating philosophy for the total unfunctioning of my former carpet cleaner.

Somerville and Ross have described a mother expounding to her son 'the nature and function of auctions even as a maternal carnivore instructs her young in the art of slaughter'. I had no such maternal initiation, but none the less I found the first taste of blood to be intoxicating. The sale that started me on my buying career took place after the death of Mrs Whatton, mother-in-law of a friend. Mrs Whatton had lived under the shadow of Inkpen Beacon near Ham Spray, the house Ralph and Frances Partridge had inherited from Lytton Strachey. It was here that we stayed in our early married days, when I was ever grateful to Partridge for teaching me to make mayonnaise.

In the marquee erected for the auction there was a cluster of near neighbours, Ralph and Frances Partridge, not seen for twenty years when we had played wild croquet on their lawn, and Mary Campbell, a contemporary of mine, with her daughters, Serena and Nell Dunn. This party went off to find some food, just before a lot of five Parian busts of railway engineers came up for sale, Stephenson and Gooch among them. The library of my family's home in Ireland had the tops of the bookshelves ornamented by busts of poets and philosophers, and this had always seemed to me correct for a library. Railway engineers were sacred to me, as from childhood I had been fascinated by the trains which ran through the Cherwell valley below our English home. Dealers, at least out of town, had not yet caught up with the rising tide of interest in Victorian artefacts. This ignorance, which soon evaporated, operated in my favour. The lot was called. There was a pause, then a voice, which sounded like that of an auctioneer's stooge, called 'Ten shillings'. Unversed in the practice of advancing by percentages, I called 'A pound' and, there being no opposition, became possessed of five examples of the work of the family of Wyon. Margaret, their late owner's daughter-in-law, thought the busts were connected with an interest the Whatton family had in the early development of railways. This conjures up a pleasing picture of the Chairman clearing his throat and announcing that though the dividend would be passed, there would be a distribution of busts. Ralph Partridge was reported to be disappointed at missing this bargain, but I still think that Stephenson and his peers look happier against the Edward Bawden stripes of our library wallpaper than they would have done against the mustard-and-aubergine colour scheme bequeathed by Bloomsbury to Hamspray.

Desmond Coke, in *Confessions of an Incurable Collector*, made the rather *parti pris* statement that it was untrue that married men had no time to be collectors – collectors had no time to marry. Coke might have added that collections do not grow, they breed. In my case the engineers were joined by a bust of the revivalist Spurgeon, whose buttoned waistcoats and bow tie slightly spoilt the uniformity of the engineers' draped togas. Queen Alexandra, in all the magic of the beauty which Tennyson saluted in 'Sea-King's daughter from over the foam', was in perfect condition when I found her for only fifteen shillings in a Frome shop.

Unfortunately, a large oil painting said to have been of the first Duke of Marlborough decapitated her, and her purity of outline was never quite regained.

The beautiful princess was joined by her sister-in-law Princess Louise and her husband, Marquess of Lorne and later Duke of Argyll. They were cast in terracotta, and fortunately the legends *P. Louise* and *Lorne* meant little to the dealer in the Portobello Road from whom I bought them. The couple had lived, rather unhappily, in Kensington Palace. A statue of Louise's mother, Queen Victoria, sculpted on a smaller scale by Louise herself and then enlarged, stands just outside in Kensington Gardens. J. M. Barrie, by whom Kensington Gardens was turned into a world of somewhat sinister magic, called the statue the Big Penny, since Queen Victoria represented pennies to a Victorian child. My collection of small royal busts, begun accidentally, was completed by the Empress Eugenie, whose long, thin nose and elegantly styled hair was, I think, unrecognised by the dealers at a sale in Frome. If Charlotte M. Yonge is to be believed, the Empress's way with her hair was known in some British circles as 'Huggeny'. Although the enjoyment of bidding at auctions might be condemned as materialism spiced by gambling, I have always found that defeats fade and victories bring their own trophies as reminders.

During our second summer (1953) at Chantry the neighbourhood rallied round a sale of far richer potential than the one at which I had bought the railway engineers. Babington House, now inhabited by Monica and Anthony Jennings, parents of an enjoyably large family, had until 1951 been in the solitary occupation of the widowed Mrs Knatchbull, a gifted pianist much loved by her neighbours.

As a young student in London, Mrs Knatchbull had helped to finance her studies by playing popular music at parties given by a hostess whose reputation was slightly suspect. Captain Wyndham Knatchbull, late Third Dragoons, would come up from Somerset and attend these evenings. Dora Estella Bright would play the piano, and it must be added that there was no shadow on Miss Bright's reputation. Nevertheless, Captain Knatchbull's family were taken aback when, at the age of sixty-three, he married Miss Bright, about forty years his junior. Eight years later he died and his widow came into possession of Babington House, where she reigned for the next half-century. Her musical entertainments were of a quality far superior to many to be found in big cities and her neighbours recognised how lucky they were.

Meanwhile, the house became increasingly fossilised. Sir Orme Sergeant (famous as 'Moley' in the Foreign Office) told me of the shock he had had on retiring for a siesta as a guest of Mrs Knatchbull. He pulled down the blind of his bedroom window and a bombshell of flies, undisturbed for years, broke over his head. Mrs Knatchbull herself was an enthusiastic bidder at auctions. Cases would arrive from Sotheby's or Christie's, the contents sometimes retaining their labels, with lot numbers, as they stood on window-sills or chests. It was far from unknown for the cases to remain intact as they had arrived. The final sale at Babington had thus an element of a Lucky Dip.

Under a brilliant August sun crowds, local and beyond, rallied at Babington. The church stands only a hundred yards from the house, a perfect unrestored example of the architecture of 1747 with the arms of King George the Second displaying the White Horse of Hanover. Outside, tombs of previous owners lie scattered in the turf. It was a perfect setting for what holiday brochures call 'an outing for the family'. Picnics were eaten, drinks poured and babies in push-chairs received, as it were, a baptism of fire. When some elegant but rather frail library steps came up for sale Percy Quick, the famous Frome auctioneer, suggested five pounds as a start. There were no bids and, thinking that someone would like them, I nodded at three pounds. I did not even need to take them home as Mr Pattimore, antique dealer from Somerton, willingly gave me five pounds.

Although The Chantry was still far from fully furnished, these adventures at auctions helped to reduce the pangs, 'to arrive is to die a little', inevitable when a family moves. There was a sensation that we had become *embrigadé*. It was not, however, until 1956 that a sale took place which afforded the opportunity to turn the old kitchen in the basement into a billiard room. As tide-marks in the years I should mention that *The Acceptance World* (1955) was to be followed by *At Lady Molly's* (1957), which carried Nicholas Jenkins, the narrator of *Dance*, to the moment of his marriage, while for his former school fellow Widmerpool was reserved a grisly failure to achieve matrimony.

Taking Anthony to Westbury Station in the early summer of 1956 I noticed that a sale was advertised at Cradlebridge, a house barely visible behind thick trees and high walls. Exploring this prospect, I found what can only be called a time capsule, a house in which the owner, a collector of pictures, had died, like Mrs Knatchbull, with his treasures mouldering around him. My eye was caught by a water-colour of a lady in a mantilla, plucking the strings of a guitar.

Like a hound going into covert, I snuffled through the other items in the catalogue and at the sale itself accomplished a wonderful day's shopping. I did not bid for any of the Rowlandsons on offer, as I happened to possess Desmond Coke's *Confessions of an Incurable Collector*, mentioned earlier, which had taught me that only too often signatures in ink of a later date, faded to a different shade, could identify a supposed Rowlandson as being of doubtful authenticity. I had, however, a friend who was kind enough to bid for me with great success, when I was obliged to leave the sale to attend the funeral of Mrs Maydwell, my nearest neighbour in Chantry. Consequently, I became possessed of the lady with the guitar, a small oil of a trooper in the Second Life Guards, my father's regiment, various engravings including two by Leech and a small but sturdy billiard table, complete with cues, a cue rack and the coloured balls needed for a game of 'slosh'. The total outlay, if I remember rightly, was about twenty pounds, which could not be called extravagant, particularly as the billiard table is still in play.

My only foray into what might be called the big time at auction sales took place at Sotheby's in the summer of 1959, when I was looking for an Empire bed, Anthony's request as a silver wedding present. I left a bid for fifty pounds, but had an appointment for some dreary work at our then dentist. I confided my preoccupation to him, and very sportingly he bustled through the filling and urged me to hurry back to Bond Street. My nerves were shaken, even more than usual on such occasions, by the sight of two obvious competitors actually sitting on the bed that was my object. Additionally, the Rubens of the *Adoration of the Kings*, now hanging in the chapel of King's College,

Cambridge, was displayed on the wall behind the bed. I was terrified that I might have muddled the lot numbers and would find myself bidding for this masterpiece, which, incidentally, went for a world record price never before achieved by a picture sold at auction. The bidding for the Empire bed rose from forty pounds to sixty-four, when I joined in, dropping out at seventy-four pounds, refusing at seventy-eight and nodding at the last moment for eighty pounds. When the bed was knocked down to me I thought I was going to faint, but as my sister, Mary Clive, also in the sale room, never realised that I had rushed back from the dentist's chair there must, I think, have been a touch of professionalism in my behaviour. The Empire bed celebrated twenty-five years of marriage and distinctly raised the tone of bedroom furniture at The Chantry.

For a silver wedding present to me, Anthony had discovered a particularly charming chalk drawing, the rear view of a tall, elegant lady in a dress which emphasised the lines of her back. The drawing has never ceased to give me pleasure, and the lady's sexual attraction once drew a loud wolf whistle from a school friend of John's.

III
New Life, Old Houses

When we moved to Somerset it became possible to dispatch the boys by train from Bristol to Hereford, to stay with my sister Mary Clive at Whitfield. Her husband, Meysey, had been killed in Tunisia in 1943, and she had been left with two children, George and Alice, younger than Tristram but older than John. Their home was beautiful, but somewhat remote as to neighbours with children of suitable ages. To fetch the boys home after these visits I would drive across the Cotswolds and invite myself to break the journey at Stinchcombe, near Dursley, where Laura and Evelyn Waugh were living at that time.

The visit I remember most clearly was in the dog days of August. Stinchcombe had become isolated from open country behind it by the onward march of industrial Dursley. On the other hand the view across the Severn towards the Welsh mountains remained as ever romantic. Evelyn was wearing a check suit and, when out of doors, his grey bowler (know as 'white' in the trade). To this outfit, more suitable for a smart race meeting than a stroll in the garden, he had added a cigar as an extra stage property. Thus kitted out, Evelyn came to say goodbye, five or six children crowding as close as was consistent with keeping a weather eye on their father. It was then that he protested to Laura that Septimus, his youngest son, was running about without a shirt. He himself, Evelyn said, had been brought up in a modest home, but it had never been in a state of *sans chemise*. I suggested that however modest the Waughs' Hampstead home had been, I was sure that someone had been employed solely to look after Evelyn and probably someone else had come in to do the child's washing. On reflection, Evelyn admitted that this was the case, which was handsome in the circumstances.

He then turned to his children. 'Shall we', he said, 'give you to Lady Violet to take away?' This ancient parental jest is usually greeted with screams of protest by the children concerned. The younger Waughs, however, showed an unexpected keenness to take the suggestion seriously. Our then motor car was the aged Humber (it would, as I have said, now be a valuable antique) but, ignoring its unfashionable resemblance to a village station taxi, the children began to scramble into the back.

On the flats of the Severn below Stinchcombe it was possible in clear weather to see the outline of Berkeley Castle. Evelyn took a proprietary interest in this fortress where King Edward the Second met his grisly death, the Berkeley family measuring up to his ideal of aristocratic Roman Catholics. Knowing this, I once unkindly laid a trap for him, into which he fell with both feet. After the Waughs had moved to Combe Florey, and Taunton had become their station, Evelyn joined the happy brotherhood of those who travel on the line from Paddington to Plymouth.

Anthony and I happened to meet Evelyn in the restaurant car, and we settled down to have luncheon together. As the train got up steam and pulled out of the station I remarked, bowling for a catch, 'I have just seen the Earl of Berkeley sitting next to the Earl of Dunraven.'

'There isn't an Earl of Berkeley,' said Evelyn, in the tone of one correcting a social ignoramus.

What I had actually seen was two engines of the 'Earl' class sitting gently puffing side by side.

As our first full year at Chantry drew to a close, the pattern of life began to settle down. There had been a horrible scare when Tristram was rushed to a Bath nursing home with what the specialist described as 'a pig of an ear', but he made so good a recovery that he only missed two weeks of his second half at Eton. Life as Eton parents became spectacularly easier when Karen and Osbert Lancaster moved to Leicester House, at the end of the Fairmile outside Henley-on-Thames. Technically, this may have been beyond the permitted limit for taking out boys from Eton, but the authorities had learnt to turn a blind eye.

Leicester House suited the tastes of both the Lancasters almost miraculously. Osbert might have been called a master of social gregariousness; with a house on a main artery leading to Oxford and points west, he could be confident of a steady flow of callers. Neighbours, also, were congenial: Stonors, Flemings, Hart-Davises and above all the John Pipers at Fawley Bottom. These last were the friends that lured even Karen from her own fireside to evenings when John Piper played the songs of the twenties and thirties to a chorus of mixed – very mixed – voices of the dinner guests.

Building development has now spread over the site of Leicester House and over the garden where giant ilex trees hid both the croquet lawn and the hard tennis court. It was in this garden that Karen, with only ten years before her lamented death, would walk out with a basket of grain for the black and white pigeons. Artists' possessions often take on the characteristics of their owners' works. These birds always looked as if they had been designed by Osbert, who in any case found pigeons useful in his cartoons for expressing opinions. Karen would welcome visitors, but was highly selective about the social occasions she was prepared to patronise. It was with the Pipers that she felt at her happiest, and it is in Fawley churchyard that she is buried.

My absorption into a new life in the country was interrupted by visits to London, one of these in order to celebrate the seventieth birthday of my mother's younger brother, Arthur Villiers. In an earlier book I have given some account of the career of this remarkable City banker, whose life out of business hours was dedicated to boys' clubs on the marshes of Hackney Wick. As his birthday approached it was decided that a dinner in his honour, given by his nephews and nieces, would be appropriate. This was deftly changed by Arthur himself into a dinner given by him, where the champagne was of superlative quality.

Arthur, a bachelor who regarded the boys of the clubs for which he so ardently worked as his sons, had taken an unenthusiastic view of the marriages of his elder sisters, but his natural reserve concealed his opinions of his brothers-in-law. I can only remember a slight dropping of his guard when he arrived at an afternoon tea party given by his sister Beatrice and her husband, the writer Lord Dunsany. In the Dunsanys' home tea in a special Worcester teapot would be rung for at intervals through the day, and the meal itself was served at four thirty sharp. Arriving at five o'clock and finding that the party had been in progress for some time, Arthur remarked in his inimitably quiet voice, 'Do you have tea at half-past four? How very middle class of you.'

The celebratory dinner party was held under the pointed towers of the Hyde Park Hotel and, besides the Dunsanys, sister and brother-in-law, it was attended by at least eight nephews and nieces out of a field of fifteen. Nephews were accompanied by their wives, but it was noticeable that some surviving mates of the nieces seemed to have felt unable to face the serried ranks of the family into which they had married. As Arthur's excellent idea of feeding his guests was to ask if one would prefer caviar to smoked salmon, the menu was Lucullan. A rather vague toast to 'The Family' was drunk, then it was suggested that a niece should make a speech. This was cleverly negatived by the nieces themselves, who cunningly called out each other's name, and after 'Imogen', 'Pansy', 'Mary', 'Joan' and 'Violet' had rung round the table the idea, mercifully, was dropped.

In a privately printed memoir of Arthur Villiers, edited after his death by Ronnie Shaw-Kennedy, a family friend, due credit was given to his active benevolence, his valour in wartime and his financial genius. Reference to the quirkier side of his character was not omitted. For example, there were the solid-gold teeth which he had obliged his dentist to insert in his mouth and which were known in the City as 'Arthur's hedge against inflation'. The gold teeth were to be seen by all and their owner would not have cared what the City, or indeed the world, thought.

There was, however, one rare confidence that my uncle made to me, a rather startling illumination of the loneliness in a life of someone admired, it might be said, by thousands. It was not long after the end of World War Two that he recollected with some wistfulness the bedroom which he had fixed up for himself in the air-raid shelter at the Eton Manor Club at Hackney Wick. It was, said this solitary bachelor, the most comfortable in which he had ever slept. At last he had had a lamp at the correct angle for reading in bed.

It was my sister Julia, married to Robin Mount and living twenty miles away at Chittern, who had originally inspected The Chantry on our behalf. Staying at the Malt House over the years, we have naturally met a number of the Mounts' neighbours.

Additionally, in Mells, just over a mile away from the village of Chantry, there lived the Asquith family, friends of my sister Pansy, and Ty Hamilton, my oldest friend from my days at Queens's College, Harley Street. Ty had four daughters, the youngest, Sarah, being my god-daughter. The request to be a sponsor came with an appeal from the baby's mother: 'Do you know any rich little boys?'

Although new acquaintances made informally snow-balled, there were also a few callers who actually left cards. Calling had played little part in my early life, since my mother had seized every opportunity to tell the butler to say 'not at home'. Her own rules for calling were impracticable for someone chronically unpunctual. Before three fifteen the household to be visited might be supposed to be still wallowing in the aftermath of luncheon. After three forty-five, it was possible that an early tea might be liable to appear. This rigid social corset impeded my mother from paying a call on a family of newcomers, close neighbours, until they had become veterans of village life. When I went out hunting from my mother's last country home I had to fend off indignant ladies whose cards, unreciprocated, lay mouldering in the front hall of Peverel Court near Aylesbury. No offence was meant, but some was indisputably taken.

At Chantry my opposite neighbour, Mrs Maydwell, combined her call with recruiting me to take over her own local commitments: Women's Institute, Mother's Union, Conservative Association. She might be said to have had considerable success, as thirty years were to pass before I was able to begin a gradual withdrawal from public life. Mrs Maydwell slightly spoilt the conventional image of her call by leaving only one of her husband's cards, pleading the difficulty of getting new ones engraved.

My next caller found me stretched on the library sofa, suffering from some indefinable malaise. No one looks at her most gracious when disentangling herself from a rug and I could not help feeling that something better had been expected of a titled lady.

A later caller, probably the last, got an even less hospitable reception. I was washing my hair in the bathroom immediately over the front door, though unfortunately the doorstep was hidden by the roof of the porch, when I heard a knock below. Expecting an engineer to repair a radiogramophone, I descended with a towel draped round my dripping soapy tresses. On the doorstep I found a lady, somewhat older than myself, with her son, who had driven her to pay this call. It was impossible to do more than accept the introduction and thank the callers for their kind intentions. These last echoes of the practice of 'calling', once both a weapon and defence in the circles where the custom prevailed, might, to change the metaphor, be compared with the dying twitches of the tail of a social dinosaur.

Having been thrown into the pond of village life, as it were, to sink or swim, I found that the two opposite ends of the village provided the poles of the community. At the one end, in what had long ago been the hamlet of Little Elm, stood the Old White Horse, where the road curves away across the Mendip. This road runs straight over Beacon Hill (1000 feet) with a view of Glastonbury Tor, sinister, magical, lying away to the south, until it descends into Wells, offering as on a plate an incomparable sight of the cathedral. Not long after we had settled at Chantry there was a General Election, during which one of the candidates said in his address that he considered Wells to be the most beautiful constituency in England. Whether from mistrust of an aesthetic approach or for other reasons, his appeal to the electors failed to get him into the House of Commons, but there was more truth in his assertion as to the beauty of Wells than election addresses usually contain.

Apart from its finale, the view of Wells Cathedral, the road over the Mendip from Chantry is panoramic on both sides. This route, along which Welsh drovers used to drive their herds to the markets of southern England, has been described in detail by Edward Hutton in his invaluable *Highways and Byways in Somerset.* The reader might well be left with the impression that from Beacon Hill it would be possible to see the Welsh mountains across the Bristol

Channel to the north-west and, looking south-east, to have a vision of the Isle of Wight rising on the other side of the Solent. Even on the clearest days I doubt if this would be achieved, but Hutton tended to swing from euphoria to gloom, particularly on the subject of what he called the Spoilation. He introduced his excellent guidebook in 1912 by declaring, like Dante, that half his life was over, then found himself revising a new edition in 1952. The Spoilation, I should perhaps explain, is more popularly known as the Dissolution of the Monasteries.

The Old White Horse Inn, Chantry, possessed a club room on its first floor sufficiently long to accommodate a skittle alley. It was in this club room that Chantry Women's Institute met, seated on seats purchased, it was said, from a defunct cinema, and so linked together in a manner which inhibited mobility. The stairs up to the room were practically vertical and, as no water was laid on, the landlady terrified me every month by carrying up a basin of boiling water for washing up the tea things. I appreciated the occasions when the WI programme included skittles, but the club room itself always gave me an uneasy feeling, as if in the days of the Welsh drovers something sinister had taken place.

Skittles were at a peak of popularity in the 1950s. The star of the neighbourhood was Willi, ex German prisoner of war, who had married an English rose and settled down to be a skittles champion. He was also a dab hand at whist, and stopped earths for the Wylie Valley Hunt, of which Diana, the beautiful Duchess of Newcastle, was then Master. Willi knocked down all the pins at skittles with such ease that he was invariably awarded a second round.

The whist drives were located in the other community

gathering place at Whatley cross-roads, in what was known as the Hut, being a corrugated-iron building bought as a memorial of World War One and, indeed, of army surplus stock. The whist drives were well attended on account of the high standard of the prizes, but there was one occasion when I was obliged to make up a table, having already given a prize. I was then required to double back on to the platform to present the winners with poultry, wines and less valued rewards. Years later, after the Hut had disintegrated, I met Willi on the spot where it had stood, he being in charge of a team from the County Council, who were erecting a temporary polling booth. Willi and I exchanged reminiscences of the days when I had handed him the first prize of a chicken, still *en plumes* and dribbling redly from the beak.

By Christmas 1953 a full year had been passed at Chantry and Anthony had been on *Punch* for the same period. *The Acceptance World*, half written, was in process of recovering from a change of house and of job, always a handicap to creative genius. My first piece had appeared in *Punch*, so the fortune teller in Albany Street was becoming ever more vindicated.

IV
Spasms of a Journal

Before the Second World War, Anthony's parents lived in 3 Clarence Terrace, Regent's Park, their next-door neighbour being the novelist Elizabeth Bowen, with her husband Alan Cameron. Anthony was luckily able to avert what promised to be a neighbourly unpleasantness. Colonel and Mrs Powell led a somewhat quiet life, which seldom included going out to dinner in evening dress, but this they happened to do shortly after the Camerons, with their lodger William Buchan, had moved in. As the Powells emerged on to their doorstep a cascade of water from Billy Buchan's overflowing bath descended on their heads and, had it not been that Anthony already knew Elizabeth, a Clarence Terrace feud might well have developed.

When the Blitz of September 1940 began, 3 Clarence Terrace became uninhabitable and the Powells resumed a nomadic existence, which they must have hoped that Colonel Powell's retirement had made a thing of the past. Finally, they came to rest in a rather charming hotel, charming architecturally that is, on the top of Richmond

Hill. I have always identified this hotel with the one in the *Forsyte Saga* from which young Jolyon Forsyte set out for a walk in Richmond Park with Irene and was immediately served with divorce papers, citing him as co-respondent at the suit of Irene's husband, Soames Forsyte.

The prospect from there in the days of the Forsytes would still have merited the title of the 'finest view in Europe', but the Star and Garter Home, built most charitably for the wounded of World War One, slightly impinged on the outlook. A telescope, however, still stood there and on a clear day a coin would purchase a distant prospect of Windsor Castle. It was in the hotel that, in February 1954, Mrs Powell fell and fractured her femur. She did come out of hospital but the shock was too great for someone in her eighties and she died at the beginning of April. I had once, in a general way, enquired if she did not find the days to pass 'melancholy and slow'. On the contrary, said my mother-in-law, they went by so fast that she sometimes felt it hardly worthwhile to get up for a day that was to be so fleeting.

Her death was a shattering blow for Colonel Powell. She had been devoted to her son, her only child, and she delighted in her grandsons, but for nearly fifty years her thoughts and actions had been focused on promoting the comfort and happiness of Phil, and to him she was an anchor in the choppy sea of a world he often found to be in a conspiracy against him. In the last months of her life he found an occupation in coping with her needs in hospital and equally when she emerged. With her death he was not only left desolate, but also his immediate occupation had gone.

While Anthony was arranging the inevitable business

that is contingent on a death, I went to London to keep Colonel Powell company on the Sunday which fell between his wife's death and her funeral. He wished to attend morning service at St Mark's, North Audley Street, where the Powells had had sittings before the Second World War. As it happened, I had been familiar with this church from childhood. Fashionable in the 1920s, the floweriness of the music and the vicar's weekly appeals for funds had led to St Mark's nickname of 'The Beggar's Opera'. In my very young days my eldest sister Pansy, a débutante, would lead a small crocodile to St Mark's, where those who did not subscribe to sittings were herded behind ropes in an outer passage. These second-class worshippers waited until the choir made their operatic entrance, lifting their voices in the first hymn. The vergers then infiltrated the goats into whatever spaces remained among the sheep. We were slightly privileged as the vicar's daughter was a friend of Pansy's. She would kindly signal to a verger to take us in before he released the waiting crowd.

Nowadays, the idea of people actually queuing to get into church must seem almost beyond belief. I can only add that in the Season gentlemen proposing to go to the Church Parade would be wearing morning coats and carrying top hats. Even before the Second World War, Church Parade had faded as an institution, owing to the increasing habit of Londoners to go to the country from Saturday to Monday. But in the 1920s, between noon and one o'clock, the broad path between Stanhope Gate and the Achilles statue was crowded both with those released from church and those who had come with the expectation of meeting friends. I do not, as it happens, know as much about Church Parade as I might, because my mother forbade daughters still in the schoolroom to trespass along the path sacred to this social rite. It was thought that she considered her children to be insufficiently smartly dressed, and not without reason, as her pleasure in clothing her four daughters was minimal and her ideas of fashion lagged behind any current mode.

These snapshots from thirty years before went through my memory, as I sat beside my father-in-law in St Mark's, North Audley Street. The bombs of war had accelerated the flight from Mayfair, no longer seen as a desirable residential area. There were many empty seats in the church and the Reverend Mr Pennyman, the incumbent of my childhood, had been followed by the Reverend Mr Thorneycroft. As we rose for the 'Te Deum' Colonel Powell lurched towards me. He was a large man, solidly built, and I feared that if he fainted from the burden of his grief I would have trouble in supporting him. In fact, he only wished to whisper that 'Thorneycroft looks old', his habitual observation on encountering former friends.

After Matins, with its memories for my father-in-law and myself, I had luncheon with him at the Rag, the Army and Navy Club, in St James's Square. From there I started to walk back to Albany, where Kitty Muggeridge, ever hospitable, had given me a bed at short notice. Half-way up the steep cliff of Duke of York Street I came upon Adrian Daintrey, the painter, seated on a camp stool and taking advantage of the Sunday emptiness of the West End to make a drawing of the Red Lion public house. Adrian had been a friend of Anthony's from his earliest days in London and remained so until Adrian's death as a brother of the Charterhouse (he was a Carthusian), like Thackeray's Colonel Newcome. I was explaining my reason for being in London on a Sunday when the rule of disruptive behaviour that attends outdoor sketching came into operation. I should mention that the Red Lion was rich, within and without, in engraved glass and was also known as the Twins to its *habitués*, after a charming pair of identical sisters whose fresh faces and simple dress were a rebuke to the garish appearance of many females on the other side of the bar. As I talked to Adrian and admired the carefully thought-out composition on which he was working a taxi halted opposite, inevitably blocking the artist's view. Purposefully, the driver strode across the street and accosted the artist. 'It is Mr Hanslip Fletcher, isn't it?' he enquired. Hanslip Fletcher was a draughtsman, frequently seen sketching in the street, whose drawings of London appeared in daily and weekly papers. His laborious technique and equivocal personality would have been unsympathetic to a painter of a younger generation such as Daintrey. Reaction to the taxi driver's question was immediate and curt. 'No, it isn't,' said Adrian, giving the unfortunate questioner a glance which would have frozen the waves of the Red Sea.

As a kind of Christmas present the staff of *Punch* were given diaries, solidly bound in leather and illustrated with cartoons which had appeared in the magazine throughout the previous year. The diary for 1954 was passed on to me by Anthony, and until I lapsed at midsummer I filled in most days. Consequently I have an unusually clear view of the early months of 1954, and with a little practice I found it possible to ignore the more banal of the drawings. Quotations and poems were usually more rewarding than cartoons, and I should like to commend P. M. Hubbard's accomplished 'Anna'. Twisting such words as analeptics and anapests to his purpose, the poem ended

Anacreontics are a kind of song
(Unlike Anna's the name of names for me)
Anna Karenina is immensely long
And sixteen annas equal one rupee.

On 10 February, to go back slightly in time, I find that I had read all of *The Acceptance World* that had by then been written. The love affair between Nicholas Jenkins and Peter Templar's sister Jean still seemed to me to be moving, increased by the ominous undercurrents which Jenkins was urged by Jean to ignore. I did not appreciate what the future would hold for the ever unfortunate St John Clark, torn between the literary exploiters Members and Quiggin. It might seem a rather fantastic parallel, but I suggested that there were early symptoms of such a situation in *Agents and Patients* (Maltravers and Chipchase exploiting Blore Smith), though in that early Powell the unscrupulous pair are accomplices rather than rivals.

The form in which I kept my diary could only be called spasmodic, events jumbled with thoughts, and chronology confused. On that Wednesday, 10 February 1954, I spent a happy morning invigilating for the daughters of my old school friend Ty Hamilton, who were sitting for the Common Entrance. It was indeed wonderful to have a cast-iron alibi to sit and read the papers, while Margaret and Sarah wrestled with questions about Pontius Pilate. To make the day even happier, Anthony returned with a bonus from *Punch*.

His wife's death left Colonel Powell desolate, though for the first few years he found, I hope, some consolation by visiting us. He had made Tristram the present of a cine-camera, a foretaste of the world in which Tristram was to make his career. John was in possession of a miniature Archie Andrews (Peter Brough the ventriloquist's dummy), a desperado with black whiskers and a slouch hat, and a teddy bear who had been in the family for fourteen years. Tristram built up from this cast what might be called a live soap opera, attended only by himself as producer and John as audience. The performance softened the pangs of the return to school, which for John was a first term at Sandroyd where Tristram had spent four years.

Suddenly, with no child in the house. I felt like a mare whose foal had been taken to market. It was now that we began to plan an Italian visit, foreign travel having been suspended during the Upheaval, not only because of the agonies of moving, but also additional expenses, which, like a disease thought to be cured, kept on breaking out in different places. Our objective was Naples, and Sabena, the Belgian airline, seemed the best carrier, though the flight involved a knight's move via Brussels. At Brussels airport the arrangements were intimate, not to say cosy. The outdoor refreshment area was so close to the runway that passengers drinking coffee were warned to keep their heads down when the wing of an incoming aircraft swept past.

The perils seem, in retrospect, hardly less remote than Stendhal's account of his travels from Rome to Naples one hundred and forty-three years earlier. Of course, the trick of leaving an apparently dead man lying in the road (and even if the corpse was ignored the robber gang could still contrive to halt the carriage) was no longer practised. There was, however, a moment on the cliff road between Amalfi and Sorrento when a shout of protest came from the back of a Cook's tour coach. A passenger from Texas yelled an enquiry as to what the crazy driver up front thought he was doing. He obviously felt that the dangers of Italian travel were still a threat. Incidentally, an hotel in Sorrento, in 1954, by some printing error, offered 'IXth century Comfort' to its patrons.

The Neapolitan hotel which we patronised was firmly rooted in the twentieth century, standing at the junction of the via Toledo with the Plaza Carita. The via Toledo (renamed via Roma under Mussolini) was considered by Stendhal to be the most beautiful street that he had seen, superior to the Friedrichstrasse in Berlin, on account of the better proportions of the buildings. Stendhal was also impressed by the mass of the population who swarmed in the via Toledo, a hundred times the number he had ever seen in the Friedrichstrasse, which he recalled as dominated by *'propriété, silence et tristesse'*.

Stendhal was, of course, visiting Naples when Joachim Murat was king and Napoleon's sister, Caroline, his queen. Monarchs had come and gone since then, but Neapolitans had not lost their taste for swarming in the via Toledo. In fact, it seemed to us that the only lull, at about 3 a.m., was filled with exhortation from a loudspeaker van whose top was decorated with a replica of a vast Dundee cake and whose loud hailer raucously relayed the virtues of this singularly un-Italian delicacy.

The side-streets running up from the via Toledo were familiar from Malaparte's *The Skin*, of which I have already given an outline description. Our introductions included one to a beautiful Spaniard, married to a Prince Carraciolo. She supplied us with some fascinating details as to the way

Malaparte had wrested actual events to his purpose. The Princess had herself made an appearance in the book, to which her husband was urged to take exception, but in the subsequent argument, as I remember it, the author deftly put the incensed husband in the wrong.

At one moment in *The Skin* the vast Palazzo Cellamare was described as being on fire, but when a sequence of kind introductions took us to have a drink with Ferdinand Acton no damage was visible. I believe the repairs had been financed by setting up an unobtrusive cinema in the basement of the palace. Indeed, the evening seemed much nearer to the Naples of Stendhal than to that of Malaparte. Conversation with the host in English, his wife in French and her brother in German forced me into linguistic acrobatics. The most impressive member of the family was the mother of Ferdinand Acton, to whom I was shamingly unable to offer even a few social platitudes in Italian. Introduced through a series of lofty rooms, it was surprising to meet young men in dark suits, when velvet coats and small powdered wigs would have been more appropriate. While struggling to attain a minimum of communication with the lightly shawled matriarch, there was a diversion that would also have gone well into eighteenth-century costume. A granddaughter, attended by her fiancé, dashed into the room and, embracing her grandmother, poured out thanks for a wedding present described as '*bellissima*'.

My diary note for this day ends 'Tony bravely rode up to Vomero Vecchio on the back of Dickie Winspeare's Vespa.' Richard Winspeare was the friend who had introduced us into the Palazzo Cellamare. Himself descended from a Yorkshire family which had settled in Naples, he made a valiant attempt to trace the Oates family, Anthony's Neapolitan kindred, who descended from his father's grandmother's sister. This great-great-aunt had been *dame de compagnie* to the ultimate queen of Naples. Anthony's parents had indeed seen the last known representative of the Oates family, whom photographs show to have been a man of immense girth. My mother-in-law insisted that when she called, her husband's cousin, Silenus in shape, was lying in bed under a tartan rug. By the time of our visit the line seemed to have run into the sand.

Stendhal's *Journal* gives the impression that he was keener on climbing Vesuvius than on sightseeing at Pompeii, merely mentioning the latter as the most meridional point in this journey. At Pompeii we ourselves were set upon by a particularly pertinacious tout. He offered his services in a variety of languages, to each of which we shook our heads in affected non-comprehension. Finally he asked (in despairing Italian), 'Are you, then, Martians?'

The official custodian of the more lubricious of the frescoes showed some reluctance to include me in the tour, but, on the principle that an English lady can be shown anything, we waved his scruples aside. Anthony said that the grim stone bunks in the lupanar were the most cogent argument for celibacy he had ever encountered. Twenty years later we found ourselves yet again in Pompeii, when a crowd of schoolchildren, boys and girls, were being herded through the rooms formerly reserved for *signori*.

Although our hotel had its genial aspects, we were uncertain as to what sort of accommodation was offered on the first floor. The manager was, however, a nice chap who, it transpired, had learnt English at Tonbridge, 'where I was educated'. Knowing Tonbridge as the town visible from

Somerhill, the home of the Goldsmids, we wondered wildly whether he had attended the well-known public school, but it seemed indelicate to ask. The manager made us a touching farewell: 'Give my love to your beautiful country,' he said, 'particularly to Tonbridge.'

V
Steps into Public Life

Although I had been conscripted by Mrs Maydwell, opposite neighbour at Chantry Grange, into a variety of local activities, a more purely pleasurable enlistment was arranged by Mrs Cavendish, wife of the Rector of Mells. 'This is our Rector,' said Monsignor Ronald Knox at a local party soon after we arrived, 'and the way parishes are going, he will soon be yours!' A prophecy that was to be fulfilled, with a later incumbent, in the not too distant future.

Mrs Cavendish combined a dedication to parish duties with a determination that tennis should be played on every possible occasion. She was active in organising a kind of rotating tennis tournament, matches being played in private gardens. There was a particularly charming tennis court in the garden of a farmhouse, the court itself being surrounded by a hedge of sweetbriar. At first, my partner and I were obviously on top of the match, then we began to find the shots from our opponents untakable, or rather unreachable, without sinking oneself in the prickly sweetbriar hedge. Local knowledge had directed short shots at an angle impossible to return.

The first game of the season had also been something of a disaster. Playing with Christopher Hollis, then MP for Devizes, against Mrs Cavendish and Gerald Hamilton, husband of my friend Ty, I drove a cunning shot down the centre of the court. I knew that in doubles both players would attempt to take it, but I was not prepared for the almost audible ping with which a tendon snapped in poor Gerald's leg, bringing the game to an abrupt end. A few weeks later, staying in Scotland with the Glenconners, I played the same shot down the centre of the court, between Christopher and Elizabeth. Almost incredibly, a tendon snapped in Christopher's calf, a poor return from guest to host. I like to think that in future I regarded my strongest stroke as too dangerous to be used.

Anthony was now in London for two nights a week and both the boys were at boarding-school. In consequence I had no excuse for having to stay at home with a husband or child when I was approached by Colin Hughes with the offer of filling a 'casual' vacancy on what was then the Frome Rural District Council. I should perhaps explain that 'casual' is a phrase indicating chance, rather than carelessness. Mr Hughes, Clerk of the Council, was always persuasive and I thought to accept the vacancy might give me a useful grasp of local politics. This turned out to be a wise decision in a neighbourhood where, as the fortune teller had predicted, I was leading a new life. Mr Hughes had a masterly grasp of the nuances of procedure and, at the first meeting I attended, arranged that I should sit next to the only other female member of the Council, Miss

Mortimer, a former neighbour of my sister Julia at Chitterne.

Miss Mortimer had had a career of adventure, which made my own childhood membership of the Village Girl Guides and pre-war exercises on the Thames with the Port of London River Ambulance Service appear positively timid. This valiant spinster had crossed Canada at the wheel of a missionary van and, even more perilously, had served as a borstal matron.

My refusal to be co-opted on to a rather unsalubrious sub-committee owed much to Miss Mortimer's support. The sub-committee was convened to examine the health of a large family living in conditions that a rabbit might have felt to be overcrowded. As a 'married lady', the chairman implied that I might have a more informed judgement on 'moral danger' (officialese for incest) than unwed Miss Mortimer. From her earlier career she was obviously far better equipped to deal with moral danger than I was. Miss Mortimer showed distinct signs of resentment at being labelled an unmarried sexual ignoramus, with no claims to being a lady.

While we were negotiating the purchase of The Chantry I had enquired of a local professional man if there was any prospect of a quarry breaking through the particularly charming Railford valley, through which the road to the village of Chantry passed. I was assured that no such prospect could be envisaged. A very few years later I found myself, as a district councillor, attending a site meeting to enquire into an application for a quarry extension, which would have desecrated the Railford valley and cut a swathe through agricultural land. No one familiar with local government machinations will be surprised to hear that among the ranks supporting the quarry company's application was the adviser who, a couple of years before, had assured me that there was no prospect of that particular expansion. On this occasion I learnt how important staying power is in public affairs, particularly when a committee meets out of doors. The site was exposed and the wind was chill, but I was the fortunate possessor of a sheepskin coat. As one o'clock drew nearer I was conscious that the image of the snug bar of the local hotel was acting as bait for at least one, probably more, of the party. Even the secretary of the quarry company, who had opened proceedings with a theatrical display of temper, began to compromise. I could not then know that the future would hold many such meetings, but at least I did learn that 'they will conquer or die who have no retreat'.

This was, in fact, the beginning of an era when conservation became a factor with which planners had to reckon. It moved, as a county planning officer remarked to me, from being 'a dirty word in planning circles' to something which could no longer be regarded as an agitation set up by cranks, either naturalist or architectural. Architecture was a subject of conflict equal with the conservation of the countryside, standards for council houses being ruthlessly applied to ancient cottages. There was a moment when I protested that I would gladly live in a handsome high-roofed cottage in the charmingly named Goose Street of a local village. It was scheduled for demolition and heads of fellow councillors were shaken at my folly. Should it come up for auction nowadays such a house, with stone tiles and fine interior beams, would certainly be in the six-figure category.

My diary for 1954 came to an abrupt stop on 23 June. 'Mars not so bright as last night, nor so orange. T returned (from Paris, where he had been for the publication of *Les Mouvements du Coeur* (as *A Buyer's Market* was translated) having taken in Juillard (publisher), Javet (editor), André François (cartoonist), Antonini (Count Giacomo, Italian journalist), an Existentialist night-club (where he saw Douglas Cooper), the Mayalls (Mary and Lees, then the First Secretary at the British Embassy) and Nancy (Mitford)). He had a good time.' It certainly sounds as if he did.

Although we had been with Tristram, as a baby, to stay at Pakenham Hall, Co. Westmeath, when on leave from Northern Ireland, it was only in 1951 that I had taken him and John there for a holiday. They were then eleven and five years old, and their hosts sent them upstairs to explore what had been the old nurseries. I remained in the drawing-room, with my brother Edward and his wife, Christine. The boys reappeared to say that they had found a swing in a window seat in the top passage, and there were hooks in the ceiling. Could they swing in it? Rather officiously, I said I could remember being told it was unsafe when I was John's age and had no reason to think the swing had become safer now. Edward, who resented any slur on his possessions, brushed this comment aside, and went upstairs with the boys. Edward's weight could be charitably estimated at about twenty stone, so any swing he tested could be passed as sound. When, later, I found some plaster on the passage floor I assumed that the swing had failed the test, but the matter was too painful to be referred to again.

When the boys and I paid our next visit in 1954, Edward had acquired a new friend in the neighbourhood, who appeared to feed a deprivation in his nature, a lack which had resulted from the violent Irish Nationalism he had adopted during, or soon after, his school-days. Fleeing before the advancing Russian Army at the end of World War Two, the youngest son of the last King of Saxony had made his escape with his second, I think morganatic, wife. Until then he had been in charge of the Royal Collections. According to Edward and Christine, the Princess, a charming woman, had taken many pictures off their stretchers and driven a lorry load westward.

To those brought up on Heath Robinson's illustrated anti-German book *Hunlikely* the Prince of Saxony was almost embarrassingly like his pictures of German officers of World War One. The Saxonys had bought a house called Coolamber, the other side of the Float Bog from Pakenham. In earlier days it had been inhabited by the O'Reillys, whose children were friendly with my own family. It seemed strange to find examples of Cranach (Court painter to the Kings of Saxony) on the walls, and a piece of furniture whose handles were replicas of the Oaken Crown. Edward punctiliously addressed the Prince as Your Royal Highness and parted from him with a correct Court bow from the neck. In spite of this deference, Edward afterwards said that he had been impressed not so much by the Saxonys' treasures, but by the sight of a man with a bucket actually *running* across the yard, an introduction of Teutonic productivity into the Irish Midlands.

Edward and Christine had married in the summer of 1925, he being twenty-two and she twenty-four. Pakenham, as they settled into it, had not been redecorated since my parents' marriage in 1899 and my mother's introduction of flowered wallpapers and chair covers had done little to soften an interior of the 1860s. As a small child I had found the vast four-poster beds in the best bedrooms positively intimidating, curtains, lined and interlined, making a sinister tent. My mother had always impressed on her younger children that, since the death of their father in 1915, Pakenham belonged to Edward, and only sheltered them until her eldest son came of age. She can hardly have expected that he would become engaged when barely twenty-one. In the Easter holidays before their wedding, time was spent clearing out the younger children's belongings from Pakenham. I took a rather self-conscious farewell of what had been my father's house, though he was someone I barely remembered. It was a sensible precaution. Fifteen months later a transformation had taken place.

Christine Trew had been brought up by her mother as what is nowadays called a single parent. Her father, who followed the sea, played little or no part in her life. Brilliant at examinations from an early age, Christine went to Oxford with a scholarship to Somerville. Consequently, Mrs Trew moved to a small house in Chalfont Road, North Oxford, where she kept afloat by taking occasional paying guests. I mention the house because its decoration had a great, not always happy, influence on the young Longfords when they came to drag Pakenham Hall into the 1920s.

It was not until the summer of 1926 that I saw Pakenham again. When, some time before her marriage, Christine saw the house that would be her home the shock must have been great, but she rallied and fortunately Edward was just as enthusiastic as herself to make a bonfire of the past. The pillars of the four-posters were sawn off, unlined curtains replaced thick hangings, and bare, stained boards were only covered by perilously few rugs. The young couple shared a taste for Chinese artefacts and some of these suited the rooms they were redecorating. Chinese tapestries in the Great Hall did not blend badly with the early-nineteenth-century panelling. Unfortunately, neither Edward nor Christine had any moderation in their sense of colour. In Christine's mother's home the peasant hues fashionable in the 1920s had, on the whole, cheered up a small North Oxford house. The mistake was to apply the same principle of bright crimson and acid green to the panels of the Great Hall and large dining-room. The impetus for wholesale redecorating died away and in 1954, of which I write, Pakenham's interior had become another time capsule, with the tactful necessity on the part of family guests to make no reference to objects that had become both fashionable and valuable.

It was not only the furniture and fittings of Pakenham that had become cocooned in the 1920s. On the marriage of Edward and Christine the housekeeper, Mrs Cruickshank, had remained as their cook, a position she filled to the satisfaction of all. James, the first footman from my uncle, Lord Dynevor's, staff was taken on as butler and thenceforth was called Andrews. It was later revealed that he was never christened James, but had been given the name as appropriate to his position. As a butler, Andrews's position of power increased in ratio to the diminishing amount of time that his employers spent in Co. Westmeath. Their preoccupation with the Dublin Gate Theatre and the consequent expense reduced their visits to specific occasions, such as the bluebell season and the annual school treats.

Andrews's dominion also extended over the town of Castlepollard only a mile away, where he had contacts that crossed the Protestant–Catholic demarcation line. He had, therefore, the honour of the house to keep up in the eyes of his cronies. This worked in favour of the boys and me when Andrews discovered that my sister-in-law had proposed we should travel by bus to Dunsany Castle, home of my cousin Randal Plunkett and our next staging post. With a totally deadpan expression on his sharply pointed face, Andrews informed me that Brady, the chauffeur, wished to take one of the estate cars to Dublin for some adjustment. We could easily be dropped at Dunsany Castle on Brady's way to the city, for which Edward and Christine had already left. I had long learnt to accept Andrews's writs as irreversible and so, indeed, had Edward and Christine.

A few years before, my aunt Beatrice, younger sister of my mother, and her husband Uncle Eddie, Eighteenth Baron Dunsany, had returned to their home in Kent, which had sheltered us in the last years of the war. Dunsany Castle was made over to their son, Randal, lately a colonel in the Guides (Indian Cavalry), and his second wife Sheila, known to me since childhood as her family had been neighbours of my Dynevor uncle and aunt. The Plunketts found themselves in the same situation as that of Edward and Christine in 1925, with the additional complication that Randal's father was very much alive and had no inhibitions about sniping from the sidelines when critical of a sorely needed modernisation programme.

Dunsany Castle is a fascinating house, constructed on many different levels at different periods. John Betjeman, otherwise a favourite with my uncle, brought wrath upon himself by asking if the house had been 'built by Richardson'. 'It was built by King John,' said the owner sternly. To back the claim of such a Royal builder there survived one arrow slit protected by glass, which caused irreverent cousins to suggest it was the air rather than the arrow slit which dated from the fourteenth century. Sheila's good taste helped her to redecorate with respect for earlier periods. Even Dunsany, her father-in-law, could hardly grumble at the installation of electric light. He was, however, heard to criticise the number of new bathrooms, remarking that Dunsany Castle would now be rechristened 'The Lavatories'.

Holidays in Irish Gothic castles seemed a world away from the council chamber of the Frome RDC, where I began to learn which speakers could never be trusted not to put in an oar, and which made helpful contributions. At first, I viewed with dread the strongly left-wing councillor who never failed to rise to his feet when speaking, dominating the meeting from a height of over six feet. Then, one day, I heard the late Senator McCarthy speaking on the radio from across the Atlantic and realised that my fellow councillor shared exactly the same timing when putting up awkward arguments. From then on this unconscious imitation never failed to charm. When the Chairman wished the Council a Happy Christmas I felt that we had earned one.

VI
An Acceptance Year

The Acceptance World, the third volume of *Dance* and at that date perhaps the most solid of the sequence, appeared in May 1955, but the months before had been full of incident and, indeed, drama. As Tristram now owned a cine-camera, presented by his grandparents, he was anxious to see the workings of a film studio. This was arranged by Colonel John Codrington, a Coldstreamer, formerly married to an old friend, and now in charge of travel arrangements at London Films, Shepperton, over which Alexander Korda reigned. The expedition was a rich experience. *Richard III* was in process of being filmed and we came in for a lighting rehearsal. Seated on a throne, Laurence Olivier as King Richard was improvising Shakespearean lines. He was addressing these to Ralph Richardson, who had covered the splendours of his Duke of Buckingham costume with a depressingly modern mackintosh. Richardson did not give the impression that he thought Olivier's improvisations were an improvement on the Bard.

On a neighbouring set the actual shooting of *Gentlemen*

Prefer Blondes was taking place, the scene being a Parisian night-club. I was glad to see that Carl Brisson, a favourite star of my early years, was still fit enough to bound on to the stage where two dancers, one blonde, one brunette, were going through a routine that fluttered their golden kilts. I had sat down on a handy chair and, suffering from some malaise, had begun to nod off, when I was roused by Tristram's shocked voice and a polite request from the sound effects man that I would allow him his own chair. If I had not been so drowsy I might have a clearer recollection of the two dancers in their golden kilts, one being Jane Russell (famous for her chest measurement) and the other Marilyn Monroe (famous for that and everything else).

From his nine years as a publisher Anthony had developed a distrust of all publishers' parties. I did persuade him that some of these had become more cheerful, and he returned from one to announce that he had invited Cyril Connolly and Barbara Skelton, his then wife, to stay. Jeannie, Cyril's first wife, had been a friend of mine, with whom I had shared tap-dancing lessons and we had known Lys ('our spouse' as Cyril called her) when Connolly had set up a small commune in Regent's Park. Barbara, a seductively pretty girl, was practically an unknown quantity.

The Connollys approached by train from East Kent, where Barbara owned a cottage. Beeching had not yet wielded his chopper and Kent was linked with the West by one simple change at Reading. Cyril arrived in excellent humour. On the first leg of the journey he had found his Oxford contemporary, Kenneth Clark, who had bought drinks, and on the stretch from Reading to Frome yet another old friend and buyer of drinks had been met with.

That afternoon the Grand National was won by Quare Times which Cyril, his classical knowledge slipping to the back of his mind, pronounced in the Irish manner. Luckily he had left the house before the error was discovered.

On Sunday morning Cyril set up a record of six sausages at breakfast, one still standing and only equalled nearly twenty years later by the Australian writer Clive James. Later in the day we drove Cyril and Barbara to see Wells Cathedral. Possibly with the idea of conveying peace to her soul, Cyril dictated that Barbara should sit in the Lady Chapel and raise her eyes in contemplation of the roof. Edward Hutton (*Highways and Byways in Somerset*) describes the Lady Chapel at Wells as 'the most beautiful East End to be found in England, a thing beyond criticism or praise, an immortal and perfect loveliness'. These might well have been Cyril's sentiments. Barbara's remained a matter for speculation.

To repay John Codrington for arranging the visit to London Films, he was invited for a weekend, but when he drove up to the house he found a scene that recalled the mystery of the *Marie Celeste*. I had not returned from a day trip to London, and Anthony had gone out with a local quarry owner, who was prepared to sell us a piece of woodland that would protect Chantry Lake from encroachment by the limestone industry. Codrington was further confused by the eruptive behaviour of our then refrigerator. My parents-in-law had passed on this pre-1939 model, after ours, a wedding present, had been lifted by a repair gang employed to mend bombed-out windows. It had actually exploded while we were still living in Chester Gate, blighting some indoor plants by emitting poisonous gases. After repairs and removal to Chantry the machine had developed a scream when cutting in and a loud throb, as of an old-fashioned cross-channel steamer, when actually running. The bewildered guest came to the conclusion that we employed a cook so deaf that his knockings went unheard, while she continued to beat up eggs for a soufflé.

On the following day L. P. Hartley, Leslie to his friends, brought Edward Sackville-West and Elizabeth Bowen from his house at Bathford to luncheon. Eddie Sackville-West we only knew slightly from staying with Frances and Ralph Partridge at Ham Spray in pre-war days, but Elizabeth was an old friend and, as I have said, a former neighbour of Anthony's parents in Regent's Park. It is sometimes said, in complaint, that there is little social exchange among writers in these islands, but on this occasion four novelists found themselves seated at the same table. I told John Codrington that we were companions in not having written a book, an exception which did not last long with me, nor, I believe, with him.

The Strangers all are Gone, fourth and final volume of Anthony's memoirs, *To Keep the Ball Rolling*, has a description of the grottoes, big and small at Chantry. Our literary luncheon party was taken on a tour of the lakeside and grottoes, after a reasonably bountiful luncheon. Leslie Hartley, called by my brother-in-law Henry Lamb 'the upright torpedo', undeniably found the hill, down and then up, a strain to someone of his well-filled-out figure. Eddie Sackville-West, whose face had suggested to an unkind friend a portrait by Soutine, put on a beret, which did give him more of a French appearance than such headgear usually does to Englishmen, but Elizabeth went over the course like a steeplechaser in top condition.

When a literary hostess in Clarence Terrace, Elizabeth

had taken trouble to get herself up in style, although, paradoxically, she looked much her best in simple, everyday clothes. On this warm spring afternoon she did not hesitate to tear off her stockings and plunge through the undergrowth. Some time afterwards Elizabeth's novel, *The Little Girls*, arrived as a present from her. A thread of the plot concerns a cave, sealed and only to be opened after a number of years. Shepton Mallet, seven miles from Chantry, is mentioned and I find it very easy to believe that this piece of background was inspired by Elizabeth's courageous bare-legged ramble round Chantry Pond and its grottoes.

The Acceptance World was being well advertised just before the General Election in May, but it was rather surprising when a publishing acquaintance congratulated Anthony on how well his new book – as yet unpublished – was doing, the professional measure being the amount that had been spent on promoting the novel in newspapers and periodicals. This encounter took place at the Election Night celebration given by the *Daily Telegraph*, which party rampaged through several floors of the Savoy Hotel. As results did not begin to come in until after midnight, the early evening had to be filled. On this occasion we were taken to the ballet by Pauline and Dennis Rickett, a former flat-mate of Alick Dru's in Anthony's days in MIL. Leaving the Royal Opera House, it was as well to keep one's mind from dwelling on the fact that the evening had just begun.

At the *Daily Telegraph* party there was an underground ballroom for those who cared to dance, but the action was mostly round the screens where the results came in and champagne flowed as from a fountain. There was a wide variation in the guest list, at one end Freddie Mills, still showing bruises from his last championship fight, and at the opposite pole a Reverend Canon, the paper's ecclesiastical authority. The Canon was seen to be having a restorative nap at about 1 a.m., only to reappear in excellent form at a breakfast table which he dominated.

As the night wore on, emotions ran hot and cold. At one moment I found myself soothing a disgruntled politician, who was foreseeing the defeat of his party. Later, I listened sympathetically while Graham Greene, an old friend, complained that a young actress to whom he had taken a fancy was showing an unreasonable preference for a TV commentator more nearly her contemporary. These were simply occasions for kind words, but I was somewhat foxed when Barbara Connolly fought her way through the crowd in order to say, 'I hear we behaved so well when we stayed with you that we may even be asked again.' My difficulty was that Barbara was closely followed by a new partner, George Weidenfeld, so that the term 'we' had become ambiguous.

The plot of *The Acceptance World* has fascinating twists and on the book's appearance these were generally appreciated, although the physical implications of a love scene between the narrator, Nicholas Jenkins, and his mistress, Jean Duport, caused the Irish censorship to impose a ban. Many female readers have admitted to being in love with Charles Stringham (possibly some male readers had the same weakness) and these may have felt saddened by Stringham's disintegration. Storm clouds were also rolling up in the direction of the love affair between Jenkins and Jean. On the other hand the actual advance on to the stage of Dickie Umfraville, previously a 'bad influence' in the background, introduced a character who was to be a bulwark not only of the development of *Dance*, but to the Tolland family into which he joined Jenkins by marrying.

Looking back, the summer in which *The Acceptance World* appeared has a particular poignancy, as it was the last summer when my sister Julia, wonderfully young and Renoiresque in appearance, was not yet attacked by the illness which was to be mortal. There is a group photograph which shows her to be blooming at the Eton v. Winchester Match, held that year at Winchester. The photograph was taken by Julia's old Oxford friend, Peggy Garnett, married to Douglas Jay MP. The group, besides three Mounts and Tristram, included Peggy's son, Martin, and her twin daughters Helen and Catherine.

Before I stuck the snapshot into my album I cut myself out of the group, not wishing to preserve my expression of black fury, arising from a failure of arrangements to meet the boys from Eton. I seem to have recovered my temper later, in a photograph taken by Julia in the Cloisters, memorial to Wykehamists who fell in World War One. Ferdie Mount, Tristram Powell and I stand in front of the plaque on which my father's – their grandfather's – name can be read. He had been at Winchester, as had his father before him, but he only married in his middle thirties and, killed at Gallipoli in his fifty-first year, never knew any grandchildren. That war is so often seen as a massacre of youth that it is startling to read that a man of fifty was only ninth in order of age among fallen Wykehamists.

*

Some of the dances of my débutante days in 1930 had been prettily decorated. My own had had the additional charm of a bevy of bridesmaids in white crinolines, but I never remember any party so charming to look at as the decorations Elizabeth Glenconner organised at the ball she and Christopher gave for their daughter Emma.

Under Elizabeth's instructions a pavilion was built out on the leads behind 13 Chester Terrace, only yards away from our former home in Chester Gate. It was hung with wallpaper in purple and silver, and against this background the company danced until the sun rose over Regent's Park. Flowers arranged by Elizabeth were also of a prettiness beyond the imagination of most professionals. Many grown-up children of my contemporaries were present, but I looked about to see if there were actually any survivors from the far-away night of my own coming-out ball twenty-five years before. A quartet had indeed survived: Jackie and Peter Coats, Angus and Michael Menzies. Having luncheon with Elizabeth a day or two later, and dishing up the party in detail, we agreed that these four were virtually unchanged.

Improbably, we attended a second ball in that same week, which was held in, and in aid of, the Travellers Club. We had dined with Mary and Lees Mayall, at that moment at the Foreign Office. Mary was looking particularly splendid in a Parisian ballgown of varying shades of rose pink. Sitting out with a partner, who was giving a fascinating description of a rough patch in his love life, the final revelation was interrupted by Anthony. Mary, he explained, had cut herself on a broken glass; first aid was necessary. As Anthony later described it, Mary's chair had suddenly tilted backwards. She had disappeared, her legs waving from a sea of pink frills, which had reminded

Anthony of Mrs Brown's upsets in the *Buster Brown* books of his childhood.

After these dissipations I cannot feel it likely that I made a helpful contribution to the meeting of the Chantry Parochial Church Council which rounded off my week.

Anthony has described how, in December 1944, he escorted a party of military attachés to the liberated areas of north-western Europe and so found himself staying at Cabourg, forever haunted by the ghosts of Marcel, Albertine and Monsieur de Charlus. When in Paris for the publication of *Les Mouvements du Coeur*, Anthony had made friends with the witty cartoonist André François, who recommended a pension at Le Home-Cabourg, a mile or so from the main resort. It was here that we took the boys for their first holiday outside the British Isles.

The pension stood just above the sea-shore, which compensated for the lack of a bath, although there was *eau courant* and a mercifully reliable lavatory. There was only room for the Powells and one French family. The *patronne* cooked excellently, but when the management and the guests went to bed at night it was rather as if a number of dolls had to be fitted into a box in a certain way. For part of our visit the other family of guests had a small son, who sat reading French comics with John in the freemasonry of little boys which surmounts language.

That coast is not only sacred to Marcel's first sight of Albertine and the little band, skipping over the breakwaters with no regard for the comfort of those sitting against them, but for Marcel's equally important first sight of M. de Charlus in his speckled straw hat. There are also constant reminders of the great days of French alfresco painting. It was still the practice of fishermen to load nets of shellfish on to horse-drawn carts, which carried them to the station and the train to Paris. Having caught cockles in shrimping nets, we asked the *patronne* if she would be kind enough to cook them. Slightly embarrassed, she offered a substitute dish. There had been a health warning, she explained, that people in the neighbouring towns and villages '*ne doivent pas manger trop de coquillages*'. The limitations of the warning and the daily sight of shellfish on their way to Paris suggested a Gallic wish not to warn off trade, whether touristic or gastronomic.

Crossing back from Cherbourg by an early example of a flying ferry, we set off for home over Salisbury Plain. As we passed what were then Mr Rank's Gallops at romantic Druids' Lodge, a partridge suicided itself on our windscreen and as our road lay past the Mounts' home at Chitterne we paused to flourish this trophy. The Malt House was indeed often a port of call on our way back from visits to the east. At the end of October we stopped once again for luncheon on our return from the Goldsmids at Somerhill. I was aware of a strain in the atmosphere, unlike my usual meetings with Julia. A few days later Robin, her husband, wrote to alert her family that Julia had been diagnosed as suffering from cancer of the breast. The sensation was that of entering a tunnel of which the end was not remotely in sight.

On a bright sunny Boxing Day the Mayalls entertained the Mounts and the Powells at Sturford Mead for drinks before luncheon. With the children of Lees and Mary and a couple more guests, the party was over a dozen strong. Everyone assembled on the steps outside the drawing-room, Julia took the group photograph and the sun cast her shadow blackly in the foreground, while she registered her family and her dearest friends, who have this picture as a memorial.

VII
Goodbye to Julia

My sister Julia, twenty months younger than myself, always had the appearance of a young girl painted by Renoir. In her thirty-first year, in the Sherry Bar in Pelham Street, the manager asked her if she was quite sure she was over eighteen. When it became clear in the spring of 1956 that her prospects were growing blacker, it was hard to believe that someone so rose-pink and golden haired could be fighting a losing battle.

This was, of course, a year of political upheaval. Budapest trodden down by Russian tanks, Suez a moral and military disaster, with the peripatetic figure of John Foster Dulles forever in orbit. It was hard not to agree with the often quoted commentator who remarked that 'diplomatic genius does not consist of an infinite capacity for taking planes'. It was always something of a mystery why this dedicated, if unsuccessful, ambassador for peace should have pursued his aim in galoshes, regardless of the weather.

The above more objective attitude towards Dulles was a contrast to the admiration that some earnestly liberal

British journalists expressed for Colonel Nasser. As the crisis over Suez swelled, so, apparently, did their idolatry for an emergent dictator. This went to such lengths that deep physical love would appear to have been the only possible explanation. As a final note on the career of Nasser, we happened to be on a tour of Iran when his death was announced. From the British papers it would have seemed that the Muslim world was plunged into mourning. This may have been the case elsewhere, but in Tehran the impact was imperceptible.

It was a four-hour drive to the Goldsmids at Somerhill, but once we had discovered a southern route through Winchester, Midhurst and Petworth the journey was one of scenic beauty throughout. It is so often by their jokes that one remembers and misses one's friends. Harry Goldsmid had always a sardonic, if infinitely hospitable, eye for his guests' behaviour and, on announcing that an unexpected visit for drinks to a neighbour was arranged he added, 'We often don't tell the students when to expect these loyalty tests.'

It was after a visit to Harry and Rosie in the summer of 1956 that I paused at Coombe Bissett, the home of my sister Pansy and her husband Henry Lamb, famous as a portrait painter. I found that, in a reversal of roles, Henry was himself being painted by Cecil Beaton, a near neighbour. The composition was ambitious, Henry being seated facing the artist, three-quarter length and wearing the battered straw hat to which he was much attached. Henry was interested in Cecil's use of black, not a hue of paint ever favoured by Henry himself. But Henry, to my relief, did feel obliged to expostulate at Cecil's recklessness in leaving his palate with expensive lumps of paint unscraped. I had not felt that my efforts to paint in oils had qualified me, in the presence of a Royal Academician, to protest at a proceeding which would inevitably lead to the artist facing an Himalayan range of dried paint the next day.

In that month of May, trouble was to be expected from Cypriots, disgusted with British policy. Cecil was, himself, disgusted at the reluctance of the police to take steps to deter local guns from shooting his rooks. This used to be a recognised sporting date, when young rooks had not quite left the nest, eleven being required to make the annual rook pie. The tradition did not appeal to Cecil and he resented the constabulary's excuse, 'We are very busy protecting your friends.' Those needing protection from possible Cypriot terrorists happened to be the Prime Minister, Anthony Eden, and his wife, Clarissa. They were near neighbours and Clarissa was, indeed, a very old friend of Cecil's, but he was not sure he relished the label of a PM's friend.

On the other hand we, and our family, were delighted when a letter came from 10 Downing Street to say that the Prime Minister 'had it in mind' to recommend to Her Majesty that Anthony Powell should be made a Companion of the British Empire. On the publication of the Birthday Honours many congratulations came by telegram and letter, but, as Maurice Bowra remarked in this connection, 'Those who don't write are the interesting ones.' An eccentric example in this category was Monsignor Ronald Knox, settled at Mells Manor, where Katharine Asquith lived, her son Julian Oxford being absent as an administrator for the remaining outposts of Empire.

We had arranged to import, and bottle, a hogshead of

Bordeaux, sharing the results with Ronald and the Asquiths, but as the Manor had no cellar we housed the bottles. On the day that the Birthday Honours were announced I happened to take a dozen of claret down to Mells and mentioned Anthony's CBE. Katharine looked rather wild-eyed and murmured 'Colonial and British Empire'. Ronnie Knox, with whom we were on the happiest of terms, admitted that jealous agonies prevented him from reading more than the first line of any Honours List. Only a monsignor, with no bishopric in prospect, there was sometimes a tinge of melancholy in Knox's demeanour as if, professionally, he felt he had been manoeuvred into a charming cul-de-sac.

The investiture, when Anthony received his CBE, took place on 27 November 1956. He has described his enjoyment of the occasion in his memoirs, *To Keep the Ball Rolling*. The last time I myself had been in the ballroom at Buckingham Palace had been at a Court Ball, given by King George V and Queen Mary in 1931, and a chasm of war had opened only too soon afterwards. After watching Anthony's investiture by Queen Elizabeth II, I suddenly spotted Rose Macaulay, sitting in a row below me and supporting an investee, if that is the word, in nurse's uniform. I worked my way down the rows of seats until I sat beside Rose. I should mention that one of Rose's foibles was a reluctantly abandoned idea that Anthony had married my sister Mary, author, she knew, of a number of novels. Having shaken off this illusion, Rose then mistook me for Nancy Mitford.

At Buckingham Palace, however, I was accepted as myself and Rose was kind enough to do so when I met her at High Mass at All Saints, Margaret Street, on a subsequent New Year's Day. She paid no attention to the segregation of the sexes, as was the custom at what has been called the Anglo-Catholic Cathedral, and sat firmly on the male side of the aisle. Her friend – and later our friend – Gerard Irvine was preaching on what he subsequently described to me as 'a difficult Feast, the Circumcision'. After the service I said to Miss Macauley, 'Rose, in what impeccable circumstances we always seem to meet.'

To which she replied in sharply clipped syllables, 'It does both of us the greatest possible credit.'

After the investiture Anthony gave an ideal luncheon party for friends at the Ritz. These were Harry and Rosie Goldsmid, Adrian Daintrey, Elizabeth Glenconner, and Osbert and Karen Lancaster. It was particularly pleasurable that Karen had agreed to come, for she was somewhat allergic to parties as I have said. On this occasion she was dressed in clothes about which John Betjeman was in the habit of saying, 'Oh Karen, how I love you in your grey flannel.' Elizabeth, on the other hand, someone of perfect taste, wore a wonderfully pretty turban of turquoise blue.

The party was watched with interest by Evelyn Waugh who, with his wife Laura, was entertaining, or being entertained by, a publishing friend. I was interested also to see a friend from the days when I had attended Commemoration Balls at Oxford. Even more fascinating was the spectacle, at two different tables, of former involuntary guests of Her Majesty, who had so recently given Anthony his CBE.

A kind of cumulative sadness seems, on looking back, to have hung over the spring and summer of 1956. In April came the shocking news that Charlie Muggeridge, youngest son of Kitty and Malcolm, had been killed skiing in the Alps. He was a brilliant boy, who had not long before passed top into the Royal Navy. His mother said that the pastor who buried him spoke movingly of '*cette mort, si belle et si penible*', when the boy was left among the mountains where he had died.

When my father left for the Dardanelles, from whence he did not return, he made my mother the guardian of his six children. He had also made provision for his younger brother, a bachelor of melancholy habit, to undertake this burden in the event of his widow dying and leaving children still minors. My father had, however, come to realise that Uncle Bingo was hardly qualified to make a home for a young family and, my mother told me, informally asked his distant cousin Walter, Lord Dynevor, married to his wife's sister Margaret, to act as a substitute guardian. As a character in one of Charlotte M. Yonge's novels remarked, 'No one knows what it is to lose a father, except those who have the care of his children.' It happened that only my sister Julia was under age when my mother died. At twenty, she was up at Somerville College, Oxford, so Walter's charge was nominal.

No official guardian could, however, have been kinder to his wards and, as Julia herself said when he died, 'There are so few people with whom one's relationship has been cloudless.' He died in June 1936 at his castle of Dynevor. I have written of the wonderfully emotional singing of 'Abide with me' at his funeral in Llandilo church. After the service his family and close friends followed the hearse up a narrow lane to the little church of Llandefysant, which lies below

Dynevor Park, where the Rhys family and their retainers have been buried for many generations.

Having asked the undertaker in Llandilo to provide the hearse, none of Uncle Walter's children had thought to enquire of the road-worthiness of this funeral car. In its appearance alone it could only be compared to the hearse in Jacques Tati's masterpiece, *Les Vacances de Monsieur Hulot*. A relic of the early days of motoring, it had been designed as a sort of cabinet of plate glass, ornamented round the top with a lacy border in black filigree. As the cortège bumped along the narrow track leading to Llandefysant church, those in the front car were scared stiff by the sight of the back tyre of the hearse, which was worn down to the canvas. Had it burst, no reversing or turning would have been possible. When we finally left my uncle among the graves of his forebears and those who had served them, it was hardly like leaving him alone, or indeed leaving him at all.

When Tristram and I were refugees from the V1s flaming across the sky of Kent we were lucky enough to have been offered a holiday by a friend, Margaret Behrens, who had rented a romantic house overlooking the Bristol Channel at Lee, near Ilfracombe. This chance invitation led to more visits, and to making friends with Miss Maud Armstrong, known locally as 'Queen of Lee'. Whatever Maud's hand found to do, she did it with all her might, which included adopting the Powell family. For a number of years the pattern of our summer included a visit to Maud's Hansel and Gretel Cottage, set among hydrangeas and the fuschias which make the hedgerows of Lee valley to blossom in purple and red.

As the boys grew older, summer holidays became a jigsaw of visits and in consequence 1956 was our last time at Lee. Maud, however, remained a constant correspondent, always writing for 25 April, the birthday she shared with Tristram. She particularly enjoyed describing the tea-time visits of T. S. Eliot. The poet had been brought to Lee through the agency of his affectionate friend, Margaret Behrens. Ivy Compton-Burnett has mentioned her sympathy with Mr Eliot who, if he happened to have missed tea, felt uneasy until he had eaten the meal on the following day. The deliciousness of the teas at Maud's Chapel Cottage, splits spread with jam and Devonshire cream made at home by Kathleen Rooke, Maud's cook, would have been given an accolade by any connoisseur.

The last visit to Lee was a breathing space before a turmoil of holiday plans had to be reduced into some sort of order. Mary Clive, with George and Alice, proposed that Tristram and I should join the Clives for a fortnight in Venice. Anthony, on the other hand, had been asked to make a tour of the Aegean in the company of my niece, Antonia Pakenham, Francis Wyndham, known for years from friendship with his mother Violet, and Laurence Kelly, a school friend of Antonia's brother Thomas. The cast list of this expedition changed frequently owing to a sudden engagement to marry (Antonia), another holiday prospect (Francis) and the conscience that forbade a Life Guardsman in the Reserve to leave England as war over Suez loomed (Laurence). George Clive was then struck by acute appendicitis, leaving Tristram and me to head for Venice on our own.

The doctor who looked after Julia, Ronald Graham-Campbell, was a friend and neighbour, united also by his children being contemporary to those of the Mounts and the Powells. The most sympathetic of medical practitioners, he could only warn one that this summer would hardly fail to be Julia's last. She said herself, however, that she could not afford to neglect the possible chance of a reprieve and travelled to London, where it was hoped that an operation might halt decline for a spell.

On the night of 1 September, a Saturday, Tristram and I flew to Venice, on a service that could only be called experimental. Earlier in the day I had gone to see Julia in hospital, where she was awaiting an operation on the following Tuesday. Most charmingly, Antonia had brought her fiancé, Hugh Fraser, to meet her aunt, whom in colouring she somewhat resembled. This allowed Julia to pass on a description of the wedding dress, flowing white satin and ropes of pearls, which Antonia was designing for herself, giving me the happy feeling that we still had confidences to exchange. We talked of Venice, which had been our first joint Italian experience and where we had shared a magnificent bedroom in the Europe Hotel exactly opposite Santa Maria della Salute. Besides grapes, I had also brought some pyjamas as a present from Anthony. When I was leaving Julia said, 'Goodbye, darling, thank you for the pyjamas and for everything.' When I looked back at her through the square of glass in the door of her room she was looking at me and she seemed as beautiful as she had ever been.

VIII
The Free Shows of Venice

It was twenty-seven years since I had been in Venice, but I did remember that gondolas were an exorbitantly expensive form of transport, compared with *vaporetti* and *traghetti*, though after a roughish flight, at 5 a.m. it seemed that Tristram's first visit to Venice excused extravagance. The way from the sinister terminus of the Piazzale Roma to the Pensione Seguso on the Zattere lies along the Grand Canal. At that hour of the morning there was a lull in the ceaseless water traffic of Venice. I can only use Wordsworth's words inspired by another view at sunrise.

> The city now doth like a garment wear
> The beauty of the morning; silent, bare,
> Ships, towers, domes, theatres, and temples lie
> Open unto the fields, and to the sky . . .

In Venice the fields were watery, but the vision was the same.

From entertaining many English visitors of an educated nature the proprietor of the Pensione Seguso spoke English with an accent that recalled the grown-ups of my childhood. The fact that he barely understood what he himself said, and even less what was said to him, was corrected by a manageress, fluent in English if of a less well-pronounced variety. Assuming she was a Venetian, I made some comment and was withered by the contempt with which she assured me that she was Milanese.

The fortnight we spent in the Seguso was a long war to retain two rooms and we therefore had cause to christen the manageress the Viper of Milan. Our bookings had been upset by the loss of the Clives. There was even a moment when I found myself facing a night in a remote annexe, only reached through a courtyard dominated by a battalion of those streamlined Venetian cats whose thinness has caused so much concern to English visitors.

For centuries Venetians have been notorious for ripping off visitors, but they have combined this corruption with providing free shows of a pageantry unsurpassed in any city in the world. While still arguing as to what, or indeed if, the Seguso could supply us in the way of beds, Tristram and I were swept off in a barge organised by the pensione to watch the Regatta Storica. The cine-camera given to Tristram by his grandparents had a good subject on which, as it were, to cut its teeth. The costumes of the boat crews might well have been worn by Casanova's contemporaries, but the most popular effects came from the fire floats. These, supposedly keeping the course clear for the competitors, were cheered whenever they dowsed any *motoscafo* which made a sudden dash up the Grand Canal.

It being a year with an even number, the Biennale was in progress, competing with a Musical Festival and a Film Festival, which had brought Anna Magnani, most raven-haired of film stars, to Venice. She had recently been abandoned by the director Rossellini in favour of Ingrid Bergman and she was determined to be an unfallen star. She also wished to demonstrate that, as a director, anything Rossellini did she could do better. The year before, we were told, the crowd had chanted under her window in the Piazza until she had made a positively royal appearance. This year she judged it prudent to descend to crowd level and make a tour round the Square, clinging to the arm of a chap distinctly younger than herself. Her escort had the air of having recognised a meal ticket when dangled before his eyes. Cecil Beaton, who had photographed her, described Signora Magnani as being uninhibited about 'the more private noises of the body', but among the applauding crowds this trait might well have gone unremarked.

These free shows had their own charm, but far more impressive was the annual pilgrimage of the relics of San Lorenzo, carried by boat from Santa Maria Maggiore and received at the landing stage by Cardinal Archbishop Roncalli. Surrounded by the nodding mitres of a covey of lesser bishops, His Eminence followed the relics to the Duomo, where he celebrated Mass. Filming as he ran, Tristram kept pace with the procession, while I panted after him, feeling that if I lost sight of my son, a stranger to Venice, we might never meet again.

Breathless, I was still impressed by the demeanour of this Prince of the Church and it struck me that he, for his part, was not unaware that Tristram was recording his progress on film. It was known that the Cardinal's friend, Igor Stravinsky, was staying with him for the Musical Festival, but it was only two years before this music-loving prelate was to emerge from Conclave as Pope John XXIII, when he touchingly spoke of his regret that he would never again see Venice and enjoy its musical glories.

Harry's Bar being a mail drop for many of my friends, I left a message there for Hamish Erskine, known from my earliest débutante days. Hamish had then been engaged, unofficially and unwisely, to Nancy Mitford. The engagement caused her much unhappiness, and was more like a stone in Hamish's shoe than a feather in his cap. Neither party had any financial resources, and the gap of five years in the undergraduate Hamish's favour had added to the absurdity of the situation. On receiving my message from whichever member of the Cipriani family presided over Harry's Bar, Hamish called round late at night. Fortunately, I had been placed in a bedroom immediately over the Seguso's front door and, being accustomed, now, to walking the streets of Venice in night-dress and towelling peignoir, I descended and we sat in a deserted café looking out over the Zattere. Next door to the Seguso, and a rival pensione, was the house in which Ruskin had stayed. Had the ghost of Ruskin gazed from a window, my white night clothes would have appeared quite equally ghostly.

Hamish had learnt Italian in an Intelligence job, after war service which had included wounds, escape from a prisoner-of-war camp, and a Military Cross. His work as an Intelligence officer had required him to find out whether James Joyce's brother, Stanislaus, was surviving in Trieste, but Hamish was driven to become fluent in the language when he realised how inhumanely his own interpreter was behaving towards the unfortunates who had to be interviewed.

In that summer of 1956 Hamish was something between a secretary and an estate agent of Mrs Reginald Fellowes, née Polignac, who belonged to the top layer of international smartness. With her brother, the Duc Décazes, Mrs Fellowes owned the palazzo nearest to the Accademia Bridge and Hamish had been commissioned to oversee some alterations before Mrs Fellowes arrived for the Musical Festival. As we sat drinking Campari soda in the brief quiet that midnight brings to the less central parts of the city, Hamish complained that decorations ordered in the spring for the Palazzo Polignac had not been carried out. He had, in spite of his experience of the Italian character, overlooked the need for constant supervision. Due to the resulting chaos Hamish had been obliged to sleep in the bed of the absent Duc Decazes, where he had been the victim of at least three fleas. This attack had recalled to his mind an incident which, he maintained, was the most agonising of his military career.

Among the villagers who sheltered Hamish and his companions in their escape down the spine of Italy – hospitality which might, and sometimes did, lead to brutal reprisals – there was one couple who insisted on vacating *il letto matrimoniale* for their exhausted guests. After a short pause of oblivion Hamish awoke to find that fleas of unprecedented number and agility were making a banquet off fresh British blood. Nothing that the Germans or the Italians did, he said, had compared in torment to this remorseless biting. In the corner of the room stood a large bunker in which grain had been stored. By plunging into this, Hamish managed to shake off the fleas, only realising in the morning that he was lucky not have been suffocated under the corn.

A day or two after this midnight meeting on the Zattere, Tristram and I happened to see the increasingly rare sight of a private gondola, propelled by two gondoliers immaculate in white with scarlet sashes. Hamish was seated in the centre of this elegant vessel, dressed in a red shirt and white trousers to match the gondoliers' livery. Tristram sapiently remarked that he now realised that someone riding in a gondola was not necessarily the owner. This must have been Hamish's last ride in the Polignac gondola, for his employment came to an abrupt end shortly afterwards. Mrs Fellowes's attention had been called to his indiligence when Hamish put through an early call to her in the South of France, without insuring that the Venetian telephone exchange knew to whom the call should be connected. Awakened at dawn and finding no connection to have been made, Mrs Fellowes subsequently arrived in Venice in a ruthless mood. Her last words to her former employee were said to have been, 'Well, goodbye, Hamish. I will see you next year.'

Besides Stravinsky, Arthur Rubinstein was another star of the Musical Festival, and I had, by chance, been given a clue to his appearance. The Russian musician Nicholas Nabokov was also staying in the Pensione Seguso. Having met Nabokov earlier in the summer, we drank coffee together outside the pensione, and discussed the varieties of coffee popular in Italy. Nabokov remarked that the froth on a cappuccino resembled Arthur Rubenstein's hair. Great was my pleasure when, later, I saw a figure that could only have been Rubinstein crossing the Accademia Bridge. The halo of white hair was immediately recognisable as having been lifted from a coffee cup.

After a week precariously perched at the Seguso, I awoke at 4.45 a.m. to hear the well-known tread of Anthony's feet as he came along the calle from the Accademia *vaporetto* station. He was spending a day in Venice before joining our niece Henrietta Lamb, and her friend Marigold Hunt, on a trip to Dubrovnik and Rhodes, the remaining characters of a party that had, as described earlier, consisted largely of droppers out. There was a superb exhibition of Delacroix, one of Anthony's favourite painters, to be visited and an old friend of mine, Tony Bower, had invited us for drinks in a flat at the top of the Palazzo Polignac. This flat had been created under the roof space of the palazzo and had been rented by two American friends of Tony Bower, himself of American origin. One of the guests was Esther Murphy, who had been the first wife of the politician John Strachey, and who was an admirer of Powell's novels. I think it was only later that we discovered that this quiet, pleasant, but unstriking American lady was a sister of Gerald Murphy who, with his wife Sara, had been an important influence in the early careers of Scott Fitzgerald and Ernest Hemingway. Fitzgerald based the Divers in *Tender Is the Night* on the Murphys, though their family tragedy was of a different order. Hemingway himself blamed some of his social misfortunes on having become involved with the Murphys and their lavish way of life. Tony Bower, who had brought us to the party, told me how much he enjoyed watching his hosts on the telephone, angling for invitations to parties in which he, Bower, felt no interest. The end of Tony Bower's story was a sad one. He met his death at the hands of a criminal boy-friend in New York City, an incident that might have come out of *Tender Is the Night*.

After this party Tristram and I escorted Anthony along the Zattere to where the SS *Aegeon* was tied up. Against the flagship of the Italian mercantile marine this former steamer from the Canadian lakes looked like a very small calf beside a large cow. Henrietta and Marigold were already on board, being seen off by Mark Girouard, whose career in architecture was just beginning. Neither was a big girl, but they were appalled by the minute size of their cabin. Anthony, on the other hand, had the good fortune that his suggested cabin mate, a burly six footer, had cancelled his ticket. Owing to the troubles in Cyprus the English were unpopular in Greek waters, but being mistaken for a French national Marigold, at the gala dinner, was elected Miss Greek Navy III.

Feeling some apprehension at watching the brave little *Aegeon* (incidentally still in service some ten years later) heading out into the Adriatic with a husband and father on board, Tristram and I decided that it would be cheering to visit Torcello on the following day, and as Mark Girouard was now alone we invited him to join us. I knew that, during the previous winter, Nancy Mitford had stayed at Cipriani's Hotel on Torcello, as an out-of-season refuge in which to write. According to Hamish, her former fiancé, Nancy had become so much part of local life that the professional beggars, cripples and lace-makers made no effort to keep up appearances in front of her.

Arriving on Torcello by the earliest boat from the Fondamente Nuove I saw that this might well be true. The grass-covered campo outside the Duomo was deserted, except for one small child leading a hen by a string attached to its leg and a crone of infinite age, idly toying with a piece of lace. Torcello has a reputation for lace-making, but this rather grubby strip was obviously a stage property, brought out to create the impression that *la nonna*, seated on her doorstep, was still engaged in the traditional industry.

After an agreeably uncrowded time among the mosaics,

Mark, Tristram and I made our way to the Albergo, another enterprise of the Cipriani family. Outside in the dust the iron tables and chairs were disarmingly simple and the price list on display, a legal obligation, was modestly in line with what might be supposed to be the means of Torcello's native population. Inside there was a transformation scene, chairs and tables being of the grandest style in garden furniture. It became clear that we were about to eat at the most fashionable of restaurants at the height of the season and I could only be thankful that I had brought with me several thousand lire above my normal float. Behind the spotlessly smart bar was a charming boy, of whom I enquired if an English lady, a Mrs Rodd, had stayed in the hotel during the previous winter. This sort of enquiry made at an hotel can, only too often, be greeted by a blank denial, or a grudging recollection, but on that day the effect was electric. 'You are friends of Mrs Rodd?' cried the barman. 'How is she? Only last week she sent me some newspapers.' He must have passed our enquiry on to the *maître d'hôtel*, a formidable young man with, as Nancy herself said when told the story, eyelashes of a curliness extreme even for an Italian waiter. Giuliano, as I think he was called, came to our table and made the fondest enquiries after Mrs Rodd.

On being asked for advice on what to order, Giuliano said that to eat anything except fish would be folly and particularly the fish soup was to be recommended. Humbly, I pointed out that *zuppa di pesce* did not occur on the L1200 (and cheapest) menu, the only one within our means. With a superbly operatic gesture Giuliano assured us that for friends of Mrs Rodd fish soup would be on the L1200 luncheon. It was delightful to be able to tell Nancy that her memory was green on Torcello, even to the extent of being celebrated in a superlative soup.

By now the island was overrun with visitors, and it was a relief to take the boat back to the Fondamente Nuove, and to visit the Chiesa dei Gesuiti. The wonderfully soothing effect of this church's interior, grey and white marble simulating damask, is at its strongest when one contemplates the marble curtains, negligently draped round the pulpit. It would surely be impossible for a preacher to attack, with any virulence, the sins of a congregation when speaking from such an elegant rostrum. Anything except a suggestion that hedonism should not be totally unrestrained would obviously be grotesquely inappropriate.

When the cable, half expected, came to say that Julia had died peacefully on 10 September the premonition of its contents did not diminish the shock. As Tony Bower was kind enough to take Tristram sightseeing, I had a breathing space in which to cable Anthony on board the *Aegeon*, thought to be at Piraeus. After this I sat in the Gesuati under the Tiepolo of *St Dominic Instituting the Rosary*. This church is very different from the Gesuiti, but it was a good place to grieve for Robin and for Julia's children in their loss. To myself, the loss was that of a sister with whom I had grown up almost as a twin, a close friend and the most congenial of my country neighbours, but I had also to remember the good fortune of having had someone in my life who had been all three.

Before this holiday, Tristram had been vainly searching for puppets in scale to act in the Pollock's Theatre handed on by his father, who suggested that in Venice we might find suitable actors. I sneered at the idea on the grounds that the only small dolls produced in Italy were expensive examples of national dress. What, however, was our delight to find, at a *libraria* next door to the Church of the Friari, an entire set of *commedia dell'arte* puppets, authentic in dress and the exact size needed for Tristram's theatre. The benevolent shopkeeper wrote out the names of the characters: Dottore, Rosario and so on. He seemed on intimate terms with the cast and we came to believe that it was a magic shop, for never again have we been able to find this *libraria*.

A faded Polaroid photograph, a novelty at that date, still exists showing Tristram and me sitting outside a cabin on the Lido, Tony Bower's tangled hair appearing on the edge of the picture. That morning's expedition to the Lido had been organised by Hamish, who had arranged for a friend, Signora Panza, to lend us her cabin. When we had first got in touch with Hamish, Tristram had asked me how old he was. I said, 'I suppose about thirty-five . . . no, my God, he's older than I am,' being myself forty-four. Spontaneously, Hamish told me that he had explained to kind Signora Panza that I was an old friend, travelling with a son of sixteen. When she asked how old I was Hamish had said about twenty-eight, to which Signora Panza reasonably suggested that I must be taking a stepson on holiday. Hamish and I had remained in each other's minds as moving towards middle age at a pace whose slowness bore no relation to reality.

That morning on the Lido was the beginning of a day which did not end until twenty-four hours later, when Tristram and I found ourselves having highly necessary baths in my Park Lane Club, the Maison de France. The night flight bus did not leave the louche café on the Piazzale Roma until one in the morning. Even after watching the film of *Carousel*, dubbed into Italian and based on Molmar's *Liliom*, there was still an aching hour to be filled.

Lavish to the last, Venice now provided yet another free show at midnight in the Piazza: Tristram and I found ourselves spectators, almost extras, in a film that was being shot at the foot of the Campanile. Oliver Messel, the stage designer, was also loitering in the crowd, but with what intent I cannot say. Under the arc lights an ancient, who habitually painted far from inspired pictures as tourist traps, was stretched, supposedly asleep, across the doorway of the Campanile. His slumbers were disturbed by the tower's custodian, equally aged and displaying a sympathetic manner. The artist roused himself, rubbing his eyes, then the couple tottered off together, arm in arm, amid some ribald applause from the bystanders. By then it was time to retreat to the Piazzale Roma, where we were able to rescue a young English girl from the attentions of some Venetian wide boys, who pestered her with hissings of '*Bellissima, bellissima*'.

The last leg of the journey home – Paddington to Westbury – produced its own drama. A casualty of the streamlining of the old Great Western has been the abandonment of the 'slip coach'. In those days the last coach of the Plymouth express was automatically unshackled at a distance from Westbury Station and, losing its own impetus, came to a halt, before being fetched by Thomas the Tank Engine, or a near relation, who then trundled it into the station. Of course, between Paddington and Westbury no communication was possible with the main body of the express, slip-coach passengers being encapsulated beyond the care of the guard.

The disadvantages of this isolation became clear when,

dizzy from a night flight, Tristram and I were joined in our carriage by a young man of vaguely Indian appearance who was carrying a transistor. These, like Polaroid cameras, were still new toys, and this fellow traveller was an all too actively proud owner. His experiments produced such appalling atmospherics that I asked, politely, if he was seeking a particular programme. When he admitted that he was not I explained, still politely, that my son and I had been sitting up all night on an aeroplane, so we would be obliged if he would allow us to fall asleep by deferring his experiments. I think the oriental attitude towards women spiked his resentment for, after a brief pause, he resumed the squeakings on the grounds that he could see that I was not asleep, my eyes being open. I abandoned my gentle approach and told him, quite correctly, that he was flouting the bye-laws of the old Great Western. This he denied, insisting that only 'indecent behaviour' was listed as forbidden. Being in a slip coach, no appeal to a guard was possible, but when we drew into Westbury this disobliging chap, surely a law student, leapt from the train and bolted with every appearance of panic.

IX
Under a Clouded Sky

The sturdy SS *Aegeon* delivered Tony, Henrietta and Marigold back to Venice in time for them to reach London and attend the wedding of Antonia Pakenham to Hugh Fraser. Henrietta actually ran it so fine that she was reported to have been found on her knees before the gas fire, drying the pretty dress she had worn on the cruise, just as she was due to be collected for the wedding. For the Pakenhams, Antonia's brother Thomas took photographs, while Hugh's nephew, Kim Fraser, piped, as he did over thirty years later at the wedding of Hugh's and Antonia's son Benjamin.

Public disaster – Suez, Russian tanks in Budapest – made the autumn increasingly gloomy. The unhelpfulness of the USA, to put it mildly, seemed to have been augmented by having attention unavoidably distracted from the quadrennial jamboree of the presidential election. At my bank, generally considered to be the original of Tilson's in *A Tale of Two Cities*, 'under the shadow of Temple Bar', the air stank of cowardice. In September 1939 I had persuaded this former family business to take charge of my jewellery. On that occasion one of the directors had assured me that, just returned from the City, he thought war was unlikely. Seventeen years later the same director almost hysterically wailed that 'we haven't a friend in the world', deriving no comfort from the fact that the country had survived an earlier crisis. Nasser's tactics did, indeed, enforce a period of petrol rationing, and Stalin's crushing of Hungary's attempt at freedom made 1956 a year to be spoken of by lapsed Communists as a worse experience than 1939, the year of the Russo-German pact.

Since living at Chantry we had become very friendly with L. P. Hartley, author of *The Go-Between*, of which the film, scripted by Harold Pinter, won the award at the Venice Film Festival in 1970. This success was said to have infuriated Visconti, who felt it to be an insult to his production of *Death in Venice*. In fact, Leslie Hartley had lived in Italy on and off for many years and his house, Avondale, at Bathford, a suburb of Bath, always seemed to have been influenced by his Italian sojourn. The A4, the Bath-to-London road, thundered past his front door, the Avon flowed along the boundary of his garden and the trains from London to Bristol and the West ran along a viaduct that crossed his view at eye level. Residence in Italy appeared to have inured Leslie to the cadences of traffic and train.

At Avondale, Leslie was the most generous of hosts, in a house hung with Persian silk rugs and decorated with many objects in Venetian glass. It was in a bulbous Venetian jug that martinis of infinite potency were brewed. Leslie's manservant, Charlie Holt, died a few years after we had become frequent visitors and, after the reign of Charlie, the disruptions of the domestic staff bordered on the sinister. Charlie's own manners had leant towards the informal, though usually modified when female guests were present. This was revealed to me when I happened to be concealed in a large armchair on a dark evening. Charlie entered and addressed his employer and his other guest, a distinguished civil servant, Sir Roderick Meiklejohn, in tones of jocular familiarity. Suddenly becoming aware of my presence, Charlie made a cheerful apology. Leaning affectionately over the back of my chair, he explained, ''Ullo, milady, I didn't know you were 'ere.'

It was Charlie who drove Leslie over to luncheon with us on a Sunday in December, bringing also Alan Pryce-Jones and Christabel, Lady Aberconway. This rather odd trio had stopped for a drink at Mells Manor, where they had been baffled to find Katharine Asquith alone. It was subsequently leaked that Monsignor Knox and Katharine had been apprehensive that Evelyn Waugh would be impolite to Alan Pryce-Jones for a number of absurd reasons. To avert social disaster, Ronnie had firmly taken Evelyn out for a walk, and kept him looking at pigsties till the coast was clear.

That was the Sunday when we had finally hoped to rid ourselves of 1 Chester Gate by placing an advertisement with Roy Brooks, most poetical of estate agents. He was fond of describing a small or attic room as 'suitable for a dwarf', but in our case he said that the house belonged to 'one of Mr Punch's nice new brooms'. Some friends rang in the middle of luncheon, but Roy Brooks always advised clients never to sell to a friend, and this advice we took. The final exit from our London home involved hiring a rubbish truck from St Pancras Borough Council, to the delight of passers-by, who snatched things out as fast as they were thrown on board.

After Christmas, shadowed by the loss of Julia, 1956 ended with a party given by the Goldsmids for the Chelsea Arts Ball. In pre-war days there had been one spectacularly rowdy occasion, when the show pieces, the work of art students from different colleges, had been demolished by people who ought to have known better. This was before I was old enough to join this near orgy, and by the time I attended it a team of beefy chaps had been enlisted to wheel on the decorated floats, including a country neighbour from Oxfordshire not otherwise noted for artistic tastes. By comparison, the 1956 scene was positively sedate. In fact, the most indecorous incident was the moment when Jackie d'Avigdor-Goldsmid and I toppled full length to the ground. Jackie, over six feet in height and a cavalry officer, later to be a major-general, was dressed as one of the Three Men in a Boat, complete with a spread of protruding false teeth. Dressed as a Spanish lady, my 'garments gay, rich as maybe' were hardly appropriate as a partner, and did not protect me from a number of bruises.

It seemed to be time to repay the hospitality of Harry and Rosie Goldsmid, although to lure them away from home from Friday to Sunday was hardly an act of kindness to their neighbours, depriving them of several square meals in the Somerhill dining-room. The visit was arranged for a date towards the end of March, and turned out to be attended by a series of comic disasters.

When we first arrived at The Chantry the house had only just ceased to rely on water pumped up from the lake by a rusty but picturesque water wheel. The complicated system supplied three other houses and I can well believe that the previous resident had, after she had moved, told her opposite neighbour Mrs Maydwell, 'Kitty, I miss your little voice on the telephone saying "We have no water".'

The Barracloughs, from whom we had bought The Chantry, had improved matters by linking the old pipes to a well from which an automatic pump drove water up to a tank in our roof. Sometimes, in dry weather, a tanker of water had to be employed to fill the well. The water itself was not expensive, but the tanker's hire was a figure such as only a monopoly could dare to charge. People in the village, whose smallholdings supported a few cows, had depended for a water supply on the churns they put out full of milk, which the dairy lorry would return full of water. Then, in the spring of 1957 the long-promised water main was laid through Chantry village. We watched it approaching ever nearer to our gates and, with dramatic neatness, the digging machine laid a trench across our entrance at the beginning of three days of social chaos. With care, it was possible to cross this trench, which I had to do on my way to Bath and the weekend's shopping. As I arrived in the city, our then motor car began to make unfriendly noises, which portended the collapse of the big end, mercifully outside a garage. Returning home by taxi, I found that the trench before our gates had become ever deeper. When the Goldsmids had accepted our invitation I had remarked to Anthony that I was not concerned if Harry would meet with discomforts, because they might remind him of the war, in which he had distinguished himself. I did feel that Rosie might be faced with some hurdles, and as I heard her voice directing her husband across the trench I began to feel that I had not been unreasonably apprehensive. But

Rosie's spirit survived the journey, and we spent a peaceful evening, all the more so as I have given an overall to the mother of the family who lived at the Stables. This was to cover her land girl's breeches, in which she had once appeared to wait at table, reducing the dinner party to astonished silence.

Longleat had not yet added jungle beasts and a fun fair to its attractions. It was early in the season, so we were the sole visitors. The guide recited his patter with a certain lack of sparkle, only brightening when he remarked that Lord Bath now lived in an old mill. This was Job's Mill, where we had been invited for luncheon and which had been decorated by Virginia Bath with individual charm. When Henry was told of the guide's remark he made as if to brush the flour out of his hair.

Suddenly I realised that one of the guests at luncheon was Annie Davis, the sister of Jean Connolly, the first and deceased wife of Cyril. As I have mentioned, Jean and I had taken tap-dancing lessons at Buddy Bradley's Dance Studio, a professional establishment in Shaftesbury Avenue. Jean had carried more weight than I did, but had shown more promise as a chorus dancer. This was our first meeting with Annie Davis and Bill, her husband, which led to a long friendship and many visits to La Consula (the Female Consul) at Curriana. Built in 1850, the house was Italian in style and avocados planted at that date had had time to reach the height of forest trees. Being on the edge of Malaga airport, the grove must have been a landmark to pilots in their descent.

On the way home we diverted the Goldsmids by way of Mells church, which might be called the Cathedral of the Souls, a shrine to the end of the direct male line of the

Horner family and a memorial to that family's sacrifices in the First World War. Anthony, in *The Strangers All Are Gone*, has described St Andrew's, Mells, as a unique sanctuary of the years before, and leading up to, 1914. When I first inspected the church, having lost my father in 1915 at Gallipoli, I was so shaken that I had to sit for a while to recover my composure. The ambience had something of the same effect on Harry, who said it was the peak of his visit to us.

The euphoria induced by luncheon at Job's Mill, and the emotions raised by the memorials in Mells church, were abruptly dispersed when we returned home, to find the water supply in crisis. The pump from the well cut in, but was failing to send water up to the supply tank in the roof, at least fifty feet higher than the well. It took me a week to work out that the men laying the main had cut through old supply pipes, and we were grudgingly compensated by the contractors. Meanwhile, the ancient supply tank was luckily of generous size, so plugs could still be pulled, though baths for our guests had to be banned.

Leslie Hartley was to have been included in that evening's dinner party, but failed to appear. A telephone call revealed that he had returned home expressly for the occasion, but on arriving had forgotten why he had done so. The evening was punctated by a number of discussions. At one moment I had to forbid a bet of fifty pounds, when it became clear that one party was arguing about the height of Eddie Gathorne-Hardy (over six feet) while really meaning Eddie Sackville-West (barely five foot six). When the party broke up some scars were inflicted on the pillars of the porch by a misdirected reverse from a Bentley motor car. The next morning Leslie Hartley rang to suggest making his apologies in person, but I had the presence of mind to dissuade him.

Towards the end of February I had gone over to Eton to take Tristram and Ferdie Mount, Julia's son, out to luncheon. Ferdie had passed his seventeenth birthday, but Tristram's was not due until 25 April. During an enjoyable meal, Tristram moved out a pawn on the chess board of family life by enquiring what would be the reaction of his parents to the idea that he, Ferdie and their friends Edward Adeane and Henry Harrod should spend Easter in Paris. I recognised that this was probing a point estimated to be weakest in the parent front, and also the subtle element of flattery involved. It was not thought that Ferdie's father would make difficulties, but Billa Harrod, mother of Henry, was an uncertain quantity and Sir Michael Adeane, who disliked changing his mind, had already vetoed the expedition for his son Edward.

The club that had been the Allies during the Second World War had now become La Maison de France, but it was still housed in a Sassoon mansion at the lower end of Park Lane. It was here that I met Helen Adeane, wife of Sir Michael, to discuss the possibility of her husband changing his mind. Edward was at Mr Cruso's house with Tristram, while Henry and Ferdie were in College. Another boy from Cruso's, Jonathan Cecil, was already in Paris and Helen enjoyed telling me that this trio had been known at their tutor's as 'the three cynical bastards'. Michael Adeane did change his mind, and the friendship of the Adeanes for M. Marin, Managing Director of the Hôtel Plaza-Athenée resulted in a visit organised to suit the boys' age and pockets.

The visit to Paris of these four boys coincided with a strike by the staff of the Métro, but the trains were still running and Parisians travelled free. It was difficult not to feel that the young men would be getting too rosy a view of the cost, in this case nil, of French public transport. Being entertained by M. Marin at the Hôtel Plaza-Athenée may also have set a standard of cuisine not usually within the means of young male students in Paris.

Finding that there was no reply from Nancy Mitford's telephone the boys concocted a note, which they delivered *en masse* at 7 rue Monsieur. Nancy was working and had arranged for her telephone to be rendered inoperative. As I have mentioned, she had complained that travellers from England seemed to regard her as an ever-open bistro and bank, where food and francs could be drawn on. She told me, however, that the sight of four Etonians advancing across the courtyard to her door broke down her resolution to cut off visitors. Perhaps she remembered the days when, as a big sister, she took her brother Tom out from school.

Besides asking the boys to luncheon, Nancy arranged for them to go to a cocktail party at the British Embassy. As Nancy herself came into the room, one of the beautiful Miss Jebbs, daughters of the Ambassador, was heard to remark, 'Here comes Miss U-U.' This was a comment on the U and non-U discussion, which I believe Nancy already regretted her part in promoting. The best summing up of this particular argument came in a cartoon of Osbert Lancaster's, in which his most famous character, Lady Littlehampton, exclaims, as she eats cheese off the point of her knife, 'To hell with Nancy Mitford! What I say is, if it's Me it's U.'

X
The Approach to Lady Molly

The appearance of the first three volumes of *Dance* may be said to have been milestones marking the end of life at Chester Gate and the beginning of a new life at The Chantry. The next volume, *At Lady Molly's*, was due in October 1957, a kind of climax after summer months crowded with incident. In May, Kingsley and Hilly Amis paid us their first visit, coming through the Severn Tunnel from Swansea where Kingsley was then a don at the University of Wales. I collected them from Bath Spa Station, never having met them before. I would have been devastated if the charming fair-haired couple had not turned out to be Mr and Mrs Amis. After almost thirty far from tranquil years, and a number of remarriages Kingsley and Hilly, by then just friends, came down together to see us, as welcome as they had been on that day in May 1957.

What Heine speaks of as the '. . . *wunderschönen Monat Mai*' was, in 1957, a tangle of engagements, contrasting in character. As a delegate I attended the AGM of the Women's Institute at the Albert Hall. The organisers of the movement had, in its early days, thought that here would be an opportunity for a theme song to be written by a member. After requesting contributions – one of which began 'We are a band of earnest women' – this scheme was abandoned in favour of 'Jerusalem'. Sung by five thousand voices it was undeniably a wise choice.

I was more than once a delegate at this AGM, but there was only one occasion when an item on the agenda got slightly out of hand. A resolution called for exemption from Sales Tax (a current imposition on kitchen and household equipment) on the grounds that men's working tools, tactfully so described, were exempt. At this meeting of five thousand women the Press table alone was a male preserve. I was sitting in a gallery, too far away to see the expressions on the reporters' faces, when a delegate sitting near me sprang to her feet and expostulated at the unfairness which exempted men's tools from Sales Tax.

Local government and parish affairs were still something of a background to writing articles when the wind of ideas blew through my mind, some of the latter being stimulated by books sent to me to review. Frome Rural District Council was fortunate in meeting in a handsome high-ceilinged room. I fell into the bad habit of drawing on the agenda, but I did try to restrict myself to innocuous borders of flowers. This was an attempt to stay awake and steady my concentration, though it sometimes distracted my neighbours, who would mutter suggestions in my ears.

Far less comfortable were the meetings of the Whatley and Chantry Parish Council. This Council assembled in what was rather grandly called the Memorial Hall, which as I have described earlier was a corrugated hut, an army surplus from World War One. In theory heated by two stoves, these disintegrated until councillors had to rely on bringing their own electric fires. Mercifully, the lease of the land on which the hut stood ran out just as the site was required for a road-widening scheme and all trace of the scene of so many whist drives was obliterated.

As a contrast, the dinner party I remember most clearly during that summer took place at a house in South Audley Street, with an international collection of guests. Sitting next to the host, then an MP, we discussed a supposedly haunted house in his constituency that had been inherited by one of my cousins. I dropped the map he had drawn for me on my pocket handkerchief, which was subsequently handed to me on a salver by the butler, a distinctly uncompromising missive. After dinner, in the drawing-room I happened to open a pretty Worcester china box, which turned out to be filled with pills in a variety of shapes and colours. Suffering from a cold, I took the opportunity to extract two soneryl. Later, when professional and social disaster overtook the host, this cache of pills, mostly illicit, contributed to the débâcle.

South Audley Street, scene of the dinner party where I found the sinister box of pills, ran downhill to meet Curzon Street at a T-junction. This was in the days before the Street Offences Act drove the girls plying for hire to take refuge in nearby Shepherd Market. The Curzon House Club, where I stayed, faced up South Audley Street with a fine view (now obliterated by a monstrous edifice) of Hampstead Old Church, rising from its tree-encircled hill, a crow's flight of three or four miles. At night, the view was made lurid by the number of girls who had beats in the immediate area. When I had a bedroom in the front of the club it was difficult to avoid indulging one's curiosity as to how the trade of Nighttown W1 was going. It was difficult also not to feel pity if, waking in the small hours, I looked out and saw the same melancholy figures still at their posts. A taxi was habitually parked at the corner opposite the Club, but I only once saw a couple of girls landing their catch and bustling off in it. At intervals there would be a clatter of high heels as the girls fled before the march of police boots. The police might also be summoned to clear a girl who had stationed herself on the Club doorstep, in a variety of Tom Tiddler's ground, a game when it was men to be picked up, rather than gold and silver.

On a Sunday in July, Osbert Lancaster organised a social marathon, Homeric even by his standards. I think the day started for Osbert and me by attending early service in the parish church of Henley – Karen had already made it clear that this waltz through stately homes was one which she would prefer to sit out. Devoted to Osbert, she not infrequently left it to her husband to be a social bee 'who sipped every flower'.

It was a long haul to Boughton, where the Duke and Duchess of Buccleuch were expecting us for luncheon. The most interesting place passed was Olney, where William Cowper not only wrote 'God moves in a mysterious way His wonders to perform', but also garnered the name of John Gilpin from the owner of a nearby manor house. At Boughton itself the collection of French furniture is so high class that a director of the Louvre is said to have apologised to M. le Duc for the indifferent quality of the furniture in his own galleries.

Sitting next to Walter Buccleuch at luncheon, I was in a position to admire a large equestrian portrait of his ancestor, the Duke of Monmouth, illegitimate son of Charles the Second and Lucy Walters. Unlike some of the children acknowledged by this Monarch, he was indisputably his father's son and his marriage to a great heiress gave him every advantage, except the reversion of the Crown. There were even occasional questions as to whether his parents, Charles an exile in the Low Countries, might not have been legally married. Discussing the portrait of Monmouth, I asked Walter Buccleuch if he had read a recently published book, *The Monmouth Episode*, which gave a very fair-minded account of the disastrous campaign, culminating in Monmouth's execution. As the conversation proceeded I realised that to his descendant his unlucky ancestor had actually been 'rare King Monmouth he', as in Thomas Hardy's poem, and that only loyalty to the current sovereign had inhibited the family from putting forward a solid claim to that Sovereign's throne.

From the essentially grown-up party at Boughton, Osbert drove us to Easton Neston, not many miles away. Here Kirsty, the fascinating widow of the third Lord Hesketh presided as châtelaine over the splendid house built by Nicholas Hawksmoor. The lawn was populated by a swarm of golden-haired children, among whom the then Lord Stanley of Alderley, wearing a blazer of the Royal Navy, was acting the part of a genial Captain Hook. Later, I could not help remarking that while the little Hesketh boys might think of him as Captain Hook, what Lord Stanley seemed to have in mind was the less jovial role of Mr Murdstone.

In the garden at Easton Neston there stands a handsome sarcophagus, with a flowery inscription to the memory of PUG, whose name is indeed written in capital letters. This seems to have given rise to the legend that Easton Neston was the house on which Jane Austen had founded Mansfield Park. Addicts of the novel will, of course, remember that Lady Bertram, idling over her fancy work on the drawing-room sofa, maintained a dynasty of pugs, whose sex has been the source of much learned argument. The identification of Easton Neston with Mansfield Park can be discounted on a matter of architectural dates, Mansfield Park, 'a spacious modern built house', must have been constructed a century later than Hawksmoor's Easton Neston. Similarly, the suggestion that Sotherton was based on Stowe does not stand up to examination.

The lack of landscaping at Sotherton is treated with fashionable contempt, while Stowe is a masterpiece of sweeping views. After inspecting the garden and the tomb of PUG, we went in to tea with the little Hesketh romping round us, although Peter Quennell, one of the house party, was heard to protest in a plaintive voice, 'Have we got to have tea with the children again?'

This was the summer which saw the end of Ronald Knox's life. Never having known Mells Manor before he became a resident, it seemed to me that he had strongly influenced the household by his personality. His air of slight melancholy was lightened when in search of a recondite quotation and I also enjoyed such a pursuit. He appeared to see the Oxford of his brilliant youth in terms of Max Beerbohm's *Zuleika Dobson*. Perhaps with fellow feeling for a glorious past, he quoted the description of the Duke of Dorset's features: 'those eyes that eagles, that nose that vultures, had often envied.'

At a drinks party in the neighbourhood Ronnie once

chanted what he described to me, with apologies, as a relic of his 'wicked Anglican days'. The 'relic' was an additional verse to the hymn 'On the Resurrection morning', celebrating the theory that to watch the contortions of the damned in hell is the chief enjoyment of angels. This was of special interest to me, because our vicar in the Oxfordshire village of North Aston had once preached a sermon on Bad Hymns, stigmatising this as one of the worst. Unfortunately, my mother, already distrustful of her local pastor, had chosen 'On the Resurrection morning' to be sung at my father's memorial service, so distrust turned to acute disapproval. Monsignor Knox's additional verse to the hymn was also a skit on the idea that the reality of Hell Fire had no place in contemporary church doctrine. The verse ran:

> Angels simply shout with laughter
> When the modernistic priest
> Finds the flames are *not* symbolic,
> In the least.

This fits equally neatly both tunes provided by *Hymns Ancient & Modern.*

Throughout that fine summer Ronnie's health deteriorated. The very last time I saw him was at tea in Mells Manor, when he had to be supported in his walk to the tea-table. As I was leaving he said 'Goodbye, Violet' and I had no doubt that this farewell was final, and so it proved to be. Only a short time later we found ourselves attending his burial in Mells churchyard, which was to be the resting place of his friends and co-religionists Katharine Asquith, Siegfried Sassoon and Christopher Hollis. The committal of Monsignor Knox was sung by monks from Downside.

The Rector, Mr Cavendish, much cherished by the family at the Manor, was standing by. He had issued instructions that if any of the local Anglican clergy wishing to attend should enquire what ought to be worn, the answer was 'cassocks and cloaks'. This sage suggestion resulted in a group of black-gowned figures forming a dark frieze behind the white-robed chanting monks.

At the Manor immediately after the committal I had difficulty in convincing Monsignor Alfred Gilbey, as ever charmingly voluble, that his will-power alone would not conjure up a train from Westbury Station to Paddington at a time he had decided would be convenient to himself.

Ronnie's brother, who wrote for many years under the name of Evoe, looked miserable rather than sad at the funeral. I think he was the one of Bishop Knox's family who had become a militant atheist, so perhaps the churchly atmosphere was disagreeable to him. According to Ronnie, his father felt this to be an additional blow after Ronnie's own defection to Rome. The Bishop, a man of saintly character, said to his daughter Winifred, later Lady Peck, that he was not sure that he could stand any more shocks. 'Is there', he enquired, 'anything that I ought to know about you?'

His daughter gave a gulp. 'Yes,' she said, 'I have smoked for two years.'

'Thank God,' said the Bishop, but what revelation he had actually feared has not been recorded.

Besides Edward Adeane, already mentioned as the son of the Queen's secretary, Tristram's contemporaries at Cruso's included Anthony Tryon, son of the Queen's Treasurer. Both these boys spent the summer holidays on the estate of Balmoral, where the Adeanes invited Tristram for a visit. This led to Tristram making a Scottish tour to my niece Antonia, the year before married to Hugh Fraser, who shared his mother's house on the Beauly river, and to the Glenconners at Glen, where the whole family were friends from our days in Regent's Park.

Having dispatched Tristram to Scotland, Anthony, John and I set out for a holiday at Welden-am-Wörthersee, to be followed by a few days in Vienna. The night before we left we took John, then aged eleven, to dinner at the Travellers Club, where he expressed strong approval of the chandeliers which hang in a sparkling line down the dining-room. With Schönbrunn in prospect, I was happy to say, 'You will see plenty of chandeliers where we are going.'

Our flight having landed us at Salzburg, we had time to sit in a café before travelling on by train. It was then that I suddenly realised that I should have to conduct conversations in German for the first time since leaving Munich twenty-six years before. As my earliest memories were of a childhood blighted by the First World War and the Second World War had cast a black cloud over my first days of motherhood, I was conscious of a sudden feeling of revulsion, over and above having forgotten much of the language. I did not entirely recover my equanimity until we were chugging through the mountains towards Carpathia. I felt even better after we had emerged from the tunnel that pierces the Gross Glockner, and a rather congenial restaurant-bar had produced the standard Teutonic meal of schnitzel and kartoffeln. It was then that I looked out to see snow lying along the railway line, which set me calculating the number of woollen clothes that had been packed for a holiday beside a naturally warm lake.

Earlier experience of bathing in Lough Deravaragh, had been, to put it mildly, bracing. The lake water lapped with low sounds on the shore in the best Yeatsian manner, but could only be entered after a walk over stones that would have been judged too severe a penance for pilgrims to Lough Derg. When the moment came to strike out beyond the reeds the shock of the icy water almost anaesthetised the pain in the bather's feet. My sister Julia had once been sufficiently foolhardy to jump straight in from a rowing boat, being ignorant of the depth of Deravaragh. The legend was that she took so long to reappear that her friends in the boat gave her up for lost and continued their conversation.

By comparison, bathing in the Wörthersee, warmed from below by benign springs, was a luxury hitherto unknown. The Strand-Bulfon Hotel had the advantage of a casino attached to its otherwise rather simple premises. In theory, I enjoy all gambling, while Anthony finds it distasteful, but in practice I have never cared for roulette, which happens to be the only game of chance which he enjoys. My one experience of the Rooms at Monte Carlo had been on a wet afternoon in the middle of both the off-season and the Depression, but even with this rather dim example before me I thought that the Strand-Bulfon roulette wheel was spun with a slowness approaching lethargy.

At breakfast in the courtyard, a meal which even dive-bombing by wasps was powerless to spoil, we noticed that the windows of the *salle des jeux* had been thrown open to the morning air. This I believe not to be the practice at Monte Carlo, where the heavy atmosphere reeking of past agonies is considered likely to promote recklessness in the clouded minds of the gamesters. We discovered later that this casino was, in fact, a school for croupiers, learners whose experience was gained by an initial spinning of slow wheels. Their devoted faces would not have been inappropriate for young seminarists.

Shortly before we left England it had become known that Prince Charles, approaching his ninth birthday, was to become a boarder at Cheam. His father had attended the school which, as preparatory schools go, was of some antiquity, my uncle Dunsany having been there in the 1880s. The news had an inebriating effect on Fleet Street (as it then was). Leader writers debated the value of boarding-school education for the future heir to the throne. Gossip writers struggled to wring scandal out of Cheam's blameless reputation. Cartoonists' art handled the situation with uniform unfunniness. At *Punch* the editor, Malcolm Muggeridge, crossed swords with the long-suffering proprietors in a dispute of such bitterness that the former took the opportunity of resigning.

At the lakeside bathing beach of Welden-am-Wörthersee there was another English couple with a son a year or two older than John. After a while this boy, a charming chap, invited John to play a table game of football, where puppets could be wound to dribble the ball in an improbable manner. With, as it turned out, unnecessary apprehension I wondered if John would tell his new friend that his elder brother was absent because he was staying at Balmoral and I enquired cautiously if John had learnt where the other boy went to school. 'Yes,' said John negligently. 'He's head boy of Cheam.'

From Welden we moved once more through the

mountains to Vienna, of which Anthony had memories from a visit in his undergraduate days. Two recollections had not lost their poignancy: the shattering experience in the Kunsthistorisches Museum of coming round the screen to meet Brueghel's *Hunters in the Snow* and the honour of being given a slice of her renowned chocolate cake by Frau Sacher herself. The *Hunters in the Snow* were immortal and still to be seen, and Frau Sacher's cake might be said to be her memorial.

The Russians had withdrawn from the former Imperial City, but had left behind a notably muted atmosphere. Particularly painful to contemplate was a colossal statue of a soldier of the Red Army, dwarfing the equestrian monument of an eighteenth-century Austrian general. The permanent guard posted before the Russian soldier had, I believe, been a condition in the treaty for the Red Army's withdrawal. If left unguarded, the Russians would have had only too clear an idea of what the Viennese might do to this unlovely legacy. In poignant contrast was the unpretentious bunch of flowers lying at the foot of the statue of the Emperor Franz Josef, which stands in a glade beside his palace, the Hofburg.

In my days as a rather dilettante language student in Munich I had been fascinated by Lil Dagover in the film *Elisabeth von Österreich*, which ended with her corpse, stabbed but still beautiful, being carried into the Hotel Beau Rivage on Lac Leman. A few years later queues stretched round the Curzon Cinema in Mayfair, which was showing the French film *Mayerling*, with Charles Boyer as Crown Prince Rudolf and the ravishingly young and pretty Danielle Darrieux as the doomed Mary Vetsera. This film gave a kindly view of Crown Prince Rudolf's character, ignoring aspects of his behaviour which can only be called kinky. As the high ecclesiastic required to officiate at his funeral remarked, though he need only know what he was told officially, it was probably the first time that someone in his position had been asked to celebrate a solemn requiem mass for a man whose suicide had been preceded by his shooting of his mistress. On the coach tour during which we visited the hunting lodge at Mayerling the guide offered at least three versions of the tragedy. The house itself had been turned into a chapel, where prayers could be offered for the poor souls who had died there.

A few years later I wrote a book about Maud Ffoulkes, well known for her ghosting of mostly scandalous memoirs. This book, *A Substantial Ghost* (its author being on the stout side), produced a crop of letters mostly concerned with Mrs Ffoulkes's dealings with Countess Marie Larisch. Marie Larisch was the niece of the Empress Elisabeth, whose brother had made a morganatic marriage. She became a protégée of her aunt, who was also capricious towards her favourites. By her own account Marie Larisch was tricked by Rudolf into bringing Mary Vetsera to the Hofburg, from where she was driven to Mayerling, leaving Countess Larisch to the wrath of the Imperial parents and a lifetime of failed attempts to exonerate herself.

The letters I received on the Mayerling tragedy usually announced that the correspondent was proposing to write a book on the subject, of which nothing further was heard. One offered a more than usually unbelievable explanation of the deaths at Mayerling from, I believe, a French source. At the climax of a drunken orgy, my correspondent wrote, Mary Vetsera attacked the Crown Prince with a broken champagne bottle, leaving him '*absolument châtré*', surely a difficult operation for an amateur and one unlikely to leave him in a state to shoot both her and himself.

On the other hand, the novelist Marguerite Steen told me that her cousin, a lady of the Court at Vienna, had suggested that Rudolf, suffering from a heavy cold and known to be addicted to morphine, may well have committed his double killing in a state of feverish intoxication. It seems probable that the corpse of the poor little Baroness was dressed and, in a ghastly parody of life, bundled by carriage to the cemetery of Heilingenkreuz, where she lies buried. The apt inscription over her reads that 'man cometh up as a flower and so is cut down'. This pathetic grave and the wonderful colour scheme of the Spanish Riding School, snow-white Lipizzaner horses caracoling against blue-grey walls, are two of my most vivid memories of Vienna.

On 25 October 1957 Edward Eighteenth Baron Dunsany died unexpectedly on a visit to Dunsany Castle, which had been made over to his son Randal Plunkett. He was, as I have said earlier, the husband of my mother's younger sister Beatrice, who for over fifty years had ridden out a course which would have daunted a less unfaltering spirit. My own feelings towards Dunsany had tilted wildly from gratitude for gifts of books and small boxes of snipe and woodcock together with his bursts of wit, to distaste for his uncouth treatment of my aunt and embarrassment at his public displays of gourmandise.

From his experiences on the Western Front, Dunsany distilled a book of under two hundred pages which he called *Tales of War*. I quote the opening of one of these short sketches because it seems to contain a seed from which sprang a new style of writing that, to change the metaphor, burst like a bomb on the English-speaking world. This short story was called 'Shells'. 'When aeroplanes are home and the sunset has flared away, and it is cold . . . you notice the guns more than you do by day, or else they are actually more active then. I do not know which it is.'

Tales of War was published in the United States in 1918, where the reputation of Dunsany began to grow from that date. In 1920 Ernest Hemingway, somewhat in disgrace with his parents, went, to console himself, on a fishing trip with a number of friends. One of these played the mandolin, while Hemingway, Carlos Baker records, 'read aloud from the stories of Lord Dunsany'. It is unlikely that the author heard of this fishing party, which would have delighted him, but surely the sparsely written account of his day in a battle area must have caught Hemingway's ear and set him on a stylistic path which was peculiarly his own.

Influenza had prevented me from going to Dunsany's burial in Shoreham churchyard, but three weeks later I went down to see my widowed aunt. Shoreham Station is a not unworthy stopping place in the Darenth valley, which Samuel Palmer painted as a paradise. When Dunsany knew by which train I was coming he was in the habit of walking down to meet me, usually hailing me as he turned out of the Dunstall drive into the road. On this November day I suddenly found myself expecting something that had not happened and realised that I had actively missed the habitual sight of the towering figure, the wide-brimmed hat and the wild waves of the walking stick.

*

It was in the autumn of 1957 that Malcolm Muggeridge, not unexpectedly, resigned from the editorship of *Punch*. His career in television was taking off like Concorde, soaring far above the routine of an editor, even of one who had begun to sit ever more loosely in the editorial chair. After an interregnum, when B. A. 'Freddie' Young acted as editor, the proprietors appointed Bernard Hollowood. They had shown much patience with the pyrotechnics of Malcolm's reign and perhaps felt that it would be wise for Editor Log to follow Editor Stork.

As Literary Editor of *Punch*, Anthony laid down the principle of onc long review of an important book or as near as could be found, while five or six more would be given shorter notices. The long review carried, in the middle of the page, a drawing illustrating a humorous aspect of the book under consideration. For example, Nancy Mitford, not entirely to her pleasure, was shown painting a moustache on the bust of Voltaire (*Voltaire in Love*) while the late and much lamented Mark Boxer – 'Marc' – did a brilliant likeness of John Lehmann (*The Whispering Gallery*) putting a finger to his lips at a knowing curly-headed younger self popping out of a trunk. Bernard Hollowood's own drawings were totally lacking in artistic distinction, but this did not prevent him from banning the practice of pictures which were relevant to the book under review. He was reported as saying that he could never understand their meaning, from which it can be deduced that his editorial conscience did not require him to read the review that was illustrated.

At Lady Molly's, published on 1 November 1957, was only the fourth volume of *A Dance to the Music of Time*, but could also be regarded as the first of a new period in the narrator's life. Jean Duport had decided to return to her husband and had sailed with him and their small daughter to South America. Nicholas Jenkins had been left with his thirties looming and the prospect of marriage, in the abstract, no longer something that happened to other people.

Through being taken to Lady Molly's ramshackle house, Jenkins widened his circle and finally married Isabel Tolland of a vast family of which Erridge (Alfred Lord Warminster) was the politically eccentric head. The anonymous reviewer in the *Times Literary Supplement* picked out Erridge as a new and fascinating character, but also showed perception as marking down Ted Jeavons, Lady Molly's second husband, as having promise and indeed Jeavons never fails to charm.

In a letter to the author Evelyn Waugh was enthusiastic, but said he could not have waited a moment longer for the first appearance of Widmerpool. Elizabeth Bowen also picked out Jeavons as a truly original character and, in a happy phrase, referred to 'the spoor of Widmerpool' who by this volume of the novel does indeed appear as a truffle hound rooting his way through the social undergrowth. There is a touch of tragedy in his grotesque idea that he could marry a brassy widow accustomed to living in the South of France. There was a reaction among readers which indicated that Lady Molly had not disappointed their expectations.

XI
Bringing the Good News to Aix

For the last two 'halfs' of 1957 Tristram had been Captain of F. J. A. Cruso's, his house at Eton. He had also become Oppidan Editor of the *Eton College Chronicle*. Finally, at the beginning of his last half he was elected to 'Pop' and very well he was suited by brocade waistcoats. This election resulted in gestures of respect from Cyril Connolly, whose own election he had attributed to never being seen by the bloods of 'Pop' to be associated with his fellow collegers. Cyril left me with the impression that he found it hard to believe that Tristram's success was not the result of concentrated social strategy.

At home, 1958 began with a visit from Nancy Mitford. In a letter to Harold Acton she gave a not entirely obliging account of her tour of West Country literary friends, Hartley, Waugh and Powell. Their food, she wrote, was about equal and not good, but she did add that at Chantry she was regaled with a *pâté en croûte*, a Christmas donation from Harry Goldsmid.

Nancy herself was in a rather edgy mood. She told us

that her in-laws had urged her to come to England in order to obtain a divorce from Peter Rodd. There was a prospect that a well-dowered widow might agree to marry him and relieve his chronically desperate situation. The divorce went through the courts with some rather painful publicity, but the prospective wife changed her mind. When I met her some time later she told me that she could never be sufficiently thankful that her common sense had rescued her from being the second Mrs Peter Rodd.

Motor cars still had to be 'run in' and in the Easter holidays I drove John in our new pale-blue Austin Cambridge to visit the Drus at Bickham near Minehead. Pale colours were then a novelty for automobiles, and I had even found an admirer stroking this model as though it were a cat. It was always a pleasure to call on the Drus and on this visit there was the additional enjoyment of speculating as to what we might find at the Waughs' at Combe Florey, where John and I were to spend a night on our way home. Gabriel Dru, it sometimes seemed, had never quite forgotten that it was she who had first met Evelyn and invited him to stay with her family at Pixton. Evelyn fixing his affections on her youngest sister Laura, if not exactly a slap in the face, may have left an unhealing irritation, though Gabriel in her turn had married a particularly charming and intelligent husband.

When we arrived at Combe Florey, less imposing than Stinchcombe but preferable in situation, Evelyn was toying with a glass of whisky. He felt that this was appropriate for a country squire at 6 p.m. rather than a cup of tea, or the gin and Italian vermouth which he could be found drinking when caught off his guard. He immediately offered me a glass of wine, which had been a phrase of Rosa Lewis at the Cavendish for champagne, and I was glad to accept.

John had been warned by me that his host was intolerant of even his elder children sharing his evening meal and indeed, the three youngest Waughs entertained him behind the red baize door, which cut off the servants' quarters. There was a legend that Evelyn, hearing a burst of merriment from the kitchen, had rushed through the baize door shouting, 'Let there be no laughter in my house.' Consequently I was slightly wary when it became clear to the grown-ups that John was keeping the junior party in a continuous roar, worthy of Yorick at his best, but Evelyn did not complain.

Waugh has recorded, both in his diary and in *The Ordeal of Gilbert Pinfold*, that his first warning of delusion was the conviction that the wash-stand, designed by Burges and a present from John Betjeman, had an ornamental tap which had been lost in transit. When John and I spent the night at Combe Florey the wash-stand, impressively decorated by Poynter PRA, had been installed in the visitors' bedroom. Next door was a bathroom with a lavatory that continued sometimes to flush after the tank had filled up. On the following morning John came in to report that the lavatory would not flush at all. I examined the system to find that the stopcock of the tank had been turned off. Remembering that when we had stayed at Stinchcombe the smell of fresh cigar smoke drifting in from the passage at 4 a.m. had indicated Evelyn's insomniac wanderings, I realised that though his Pinfold demons might have been exorcised, other devils still kept him on a nocturnal prowl.

*

Having left Eton with a mountain of possessions which it took the combined strength of his parents and himself to carry down to the car, Tristram had a term to fill in before going up to Oxford. It was arranged for him to go to Aix-en-Provence, the arrangement at one moment depending on the reply to a telegram: 'Tristram Powell will arrive at Aix at 6.30 a.m. To what address should he go?' The answer was chez Madame Lanes, 7 rue Cardinale, and it was a relief to hear that Tristram had arrived, with his money intact. Currency regulations had made it necessary for him to travel with the funds for his stay in Aix stitched, in a plastic envelope, into the back of his trousers, with instructions not to undress in his couchette.

Madame Lanes, who welcomed him kindly, was the widow of a general. Tristram wrote that he found his French rather rusty, but he had understood enough to be able to recount the history of Madame Lanes's father-in-law, also a general of some distinction. This earlier General Lanes had accompanied the most unfortunate Emperor Maximilian to Mexico and had been the last Frenchman to speak to the Emperor before he was abandoned to his all too murderous Mexican subjects. To have had his execution painted in a masterpiece by Manet made Maximilian's end no less tragic.

For the previous five summers our plans for foreign holidays had had the Fourth of June at Eton as a fixed point round which to revolve. John was not due to go to Eton until September, so in May we took the opportunity to drive down through France to visit Tristram at Aix. The expedition was made more dramatic by the current upheaval in France, which was to lead to the return of General de Gaulle.

'*Impeccable*,' said the gendarme at Maupetas airport, on

being shown the number of the pale-blue Austin Cambridge's engine. Then we followed the road, straight as an arrow, and happily empty in 1958, which runs down the Cherbourg peninsula, coming to a natural halt for travellers at Portorson. At the town's cinema *The Bridge Over the River Kwai* was showing and a gala display of the flags of many nations had been hoisted outside. Considering the film's theme – relentless Japanese brutality over the building of the bridge – it seemed bizarre that the Rising Sun should be fluttering alongside the national symbols of those who had suffered so bitterly at Japanese hands.

We were heading south-west to call on friends beyond La Rochelle, the city we had last visited in September 1938, when the ear had been battered by the strident voice of Hitler coming out of every radio. On this Thursday, 22 May 1958, speeches were coming from many radios, but at least they dealt with the possible return to power of *le General* and did not immediately promise a war between nations.

Almost exactly twenty years earlier the matrons of La Rochelle could be seen proceeding to Mass, wearing lace coifs of intricate design, differing according to the locality from whence they came. On a weekday it was not possible to discover if this infinitely graceful custom still prevailed. I was, however, disappointed to find that the programme at the main cinema had been changed since our last visit when *Le Sport des Rois*, with Raimu in a story of crooked horse-racing, had been showing. It was still showing when my sister Julia and Robin her husband had passed through on their way to Spain in 1950, but having kept flickering through thirteen years and the German Occupation the print must finally have worn out.

Although we made the elementary mistake of going by Rochfort-sur-mer and the dilatory ferry, we were not abnormally late in reaching the Château de la Gautaudière in the neighbourhood of Marennes. This chateau of fairy-tale prettiness was the home of François, Marquis de Chasseloup-Laubat, and Betty, his English wife. Tony had been at Mr Gibbs's day school at the beginning of World War One, where François Chasseloup, his parents presumably refugees, had also been a pupil. This was a link, although the boys had not been acquainted. François insisted that Mr Gibbs, addressing him as 'Laubat' pronounced as an English word, would tell the little French boy to bend over in order to beat him. Tony, who recollected Mr Gibbs as the kindliest of schoolmasters, found this story hard to believe, as were not a few of François's fantasies, though the dramas of his own life would hardly seem to need additional embroidery.

The family of Chasseloup had been ennobled during the Second Empire as a reward, it was said, for 'inventing rubber'. Probably this was an oversimplification of his forefather's development of a new rubberising process, but François himself had had a career of wonderfully mixed distinction. Not only had he made discoveries of ancient painted caves in North Africa, but he had written a study of the medieval churches in his own neighbourhood. Among the grotesque corbels of these churches he had found one that distinctly recalled his own somewhat bronze-like head. The wine from his vineyard he enjoyed selling to a bistro in Paris, under the label 'Château de la Gautaudière appellation non contrôlée'. Indeed so non-controlled was one vintage that a bottle was said to have burst, smashing the windows of the bistro which had offered it for sale.

By birth, François was Jewish on his mother's side – her name was Stern – by religion he was Catholic, the Sainte Sacrament being reserved in the chapel of La Gautaudière. An additional complication arose from the fact that his godfather was Marshal Pétain. (François put forward the theory that it was Franco's respect for the Marshal, acquired as a young officer in France, which prevented Franco from allowing Hitler's army to march through Spain to Gibralter.) With this birth and background, both the Occupation and Liberation had been for François a time of painful decisions and dangers.

On a happier note it should be recorded that the Marquis de Chasseloup-Laubat was a sprinter of Olympic standard, who could have kept pace with any wolf. He enjoyed showing photographs of his victories, explaining that, running so fast, he had been able to run away with Betty. She had been married to a distinguished and much older civil servant and, besides being descended from the Stracheys on her mother's side, was a cousin of the redoubtable Cara, Lady Harris, mother of Karen Lancaster.

On their first visit to London as a married couple Betty had been uncertain of the welcome she might expect from Cara Harris, on account of her cousin's disapproval of divorce, both religiously and socially. With some trepidation Betty telephoned to ask if she might bring François to meet his new relations. 'Yes, darling,' said Lady Harris. 'Now let me see, could he be a Girl Guide?' The Chasseloups had chanced to arrive at a moment when Cara Harris was relieving her recurrent ennui by organising a film production. In this she was playing two of the fattest parts, the third being in the skilful hands of her son-in-law, Osbert Lancaster, his moustache bristling under a sola topi.

The plot involved an expedition to Darkest Africa and certainly owed something to an early Marx Brothers production. Cara Harris was both the intrepid female explorer, Dame Mildred Tarchtree, and her mother, the Dowager Lady Tarchtree, who was bitten by a tarantula inadvertently concealed in a basket of bananas sent home by her daughter. The tarantula, a mechanical spider sold by kerbside hawkers, gave the Dowager Lady Tarchtree, dressed approximately as Queen Victoria, the opportunity to perform a Dance of Death that any prima ballerina assoluta might have envied. The returning explorers were greeted on the doorstep of the Harrises' house in Catherine Place by a guard of honour composed of Boy Scouts and Girl Guides. It was in the costume of a Girl Guide, complete with skirt, that François Chasseloup made his début into this branch of his wife's family.

The chateau of La Gautaudière stood in a meadow, bordered by a wood; a perron rose from the meadow and on the pediment which topped the façade the interests of the estate were celebrated by carvings of rakes for the oyster beds and baskets for the grapes of the vendange, source of the vin appellation non-contrôlée. With all this essentially French display it was fascinating to see that in the immediate neighbourhood Red Cross emergency kits were attached to trees in the manner of nesting boxes. These were due to Betty Chasseloup's organisation of help in case of accident and her public spirit had been rewarded by the tiny ribbon of an order which she wore in her lapel. I have sometimes wondered if Nancy Mitford, enamoured of French life, might have suffered a depression had she known that an English girl, married to a marquis and living in a beautiful chateau, would still be engaged in good works redolent of rural Oxfordshire.

Wayside memorials could be more mournful than the Red Cross boxes. The scars of the Occupation, ended thirteen years before, were visible in the stones put up to commemorate the brave men of the Resistance. Bunches of flowers were still placed at the spot where these men had been shot and where the memorials, heart-rending in their simplicity, carried inscriptions which told of a '*soldat fidèle de sa patrie envahie*'.

Before leaving home we had written to Douglas Cooper, art collector and art historian, for the name of an hotel he could recommend at Pont du Gard, he having settled for some years at the nearby Château de Castille. Arriving after we had set out, Douglas's letter, comparing the *confort et cuisine* of the two inns situated in the shadow of the towering Roman aqueduct, languished at Chantry until our return. As we could only choose as we found, we picked the hotel which we later discovered to be morally and politically undesirable. If I remember rightly, the female proprietor had collaborated over-enthusiastically with a German officer during the Occupation. In the turmoil of the Liberation the Resistance were able to arrange for a bomb to drop on the collaborator's premises. She, however, outsmarted the avengers by successfully claiming war damage compensation, and using it to modernise her hotel, to the jealous rage of her competitors.

A British diplomat, guest at the hotel, reported poorly of the cuisine, but we were spared sampling it. When I had rung the Château de Castille with a tentative '*Puis je parler à Monsieur Coopère*?', to be answered by a guarded '*De la part de qui*?' from Douglas, we were at once invited to dinner. At that date John Richardson, who became an equally well-known art historian, was living with Douglas and on that particular evening they apologised for asking us to share a nostalgic meal of shepherd's pie. Somerset Maugham is known sometimes to have wearied of perfect French food, and to have yearned for such nursery delicacies as marmalade pudding and treacle tart, but he drew the line at shepherd's pie. At the Château de Castille, however, a very good example was produced. George Weidenfeld, staying in the house and brought up in Central Europe, showed no distaste for a dish for which he cannot have had the childhood memory shared by Cooper and Richardson.

Some years before, Douglas had been on his way to Uzès, when on the right-hand side of the road he saw an avenue of dilapidated columns leading to an equally dilapidated *mas*, which had obviously been decorated to disguise the simplicity of its ground plan. This was the Château de Castille and a *coup de foudre* for Douglas. On that day he never reached Uzès and rather liked to give the impression that he had never reached it subsequently, any business there permanently abandoned.

Probably a hundred years before the French Revolution, a Monsieur de Castille, owner of a Provençal *mas*, a square edifice with a tower at each corner, set his heart on marrying a Mademoiselle de Rohan. To impress the young lady and her family he built a colonnaded approach to his house, flanked by two pavilions. His strategy must have worked, for he was able to encircle the roof with a balustrade linking the initials C and R. In a non-committal voice John Richardson said that, though they celebrated the union of Castille and Rohan, Douglas liked to think of these letters as a prevision of Cooper and Richardson.

The colonnades and their pavilions had proved to be beyond repair, and remained as a ruined avenue in the classical manner. In the pillared porch guests were greeted by Venus Victrix, sculpted by Renoir in one of his most ebulliently curved moods. Round the statue hoopoes fluttered, braking with their crests in the manner of a jet aeroplane landing. My pleasure in hoopoes has never been decreased by the knowledge that in China, where coffins are frail, they make their nests in the rib-cages of the corpses.

The day after we had dined on shepherd's pie, we had luncheon at the Château de Castille to meet William Fifield, an American novelist, and his wife Donna. Fifield had abandoned the lush pasture of Madison Avenue for a literary career in a Provençal farmhouse. His charming wife had given up more exciting prospects. She had been under contract as a trainee starlet with 20th Century Fox, where her room-mate in the hostel where the starlets slept had been Marilyn Monroe. Luncheon was punctuated by friends in Paris ringing up Douglas with wails of '*Nous ne pouvons pas avoir le General*', though it was more and more clear that, whether they liked it or not, de Gaulle was what they were going to get. We had rather hoped that that day would be of rest, after the long haul to the Midi, but Douglas, in a dictatorial manner worthy of *le General*, swept us off on an expedition to Arles.

The object was to call on an extremely nice boy, Lucien Clergue, who worked loading and unloading at the Monoprix in Arles, but was struggling to establish himself as a photographer. At a bullfight he had managed to impress Picasso with his photographic promise and Douglas, closely associated with Picasso, was helping Clergue's career. Later this became successful, but at the time we met him he had only recently installed himself in a bare room as a studio, using the children of the neighbourhood as models. The film *Argent de poche*, produced many years later, recalled the early photographs of Lucien Clergue. At George Weidenfeld's request I took a book of poems, illustrated by Clergue's photographs, back to London, with the idea that Weidenfeld and Nicolson might find them suitable for publication. 'What can George be thinking of?' they cried in the office. In the climate of the time it was thought impossible to publish photographs in which naked girls drifted in rock pools, seaweed mingled with pubic hair.

The supposed day of rest was by no means ended. With enterprising hospitability the Fifields had asked Douglas's luncheon party to dinner at their rented farmhouse near St Etienne des Grès. Bill Fifield took the precaution of leading a motorcade up a dusty *chemin privé* to a stone farmhouse that had once been lived in by Roger Fry. In the curious way that people bring their own ambience with them, this canyon was reminiscent of the Santa Monica Mountains above Beverly Hills where, twenty years before, Tony and I would walk in the cool of the evening. This was a transitory impression, Provence regained its magic at the sight of a man and his dog setting out for a night's truffle hunting, an ageless couple escaped from any painting of peasant life.

Donna Fifield, who complained that in the Alpes Maritimes her name was the equivalent of being called 'woman', had provided a classical French dinner, with wine to match, at the shortest possible notice. Meanwhile

Douglas Cooper, by now of ample bulk, wandered round the canyon hand in hand with the Fifield boy and girl twins. Donna, with some exaggeration, said that whenever she opened her mouth her origin as the Girl of the Golden West was obvious, but the twins, '*quand même*', as they were fond of saying, could command the local idiom.

Next day at Aix, the ancient capital of Provence, we found that Tristram had made good use of his residence at 7 rue Cardinale. His popularity with his hostess could be gauged by the room he had been allotted. Reached through a small washing place, it had a bed in an alcove hung with curtains of toile de jouy. Madame Lanes, a lady of impressive dignity, was famous as the Queen of Aix as far as foreign students were concerned. Among the fountains of Aix few can be prettier than the one decorated with dolphins which stands at the junction of the rue Quatre Septembre and the rue Cardinale, a vista closed by the church of St Jean de Malte.

Naturally, in this time of crisis, the street furniture, as it is called in municipal circles, was plastered with the claims of rival political parties, but the pillars and urinals of Aix were more largely dominated by fierce pictures of Primo Carnera, due to take part in a wrestling match. Carnera, the Man Mountain of the 1930s, had always been something of a grotesque by reason of his towering height, not, I believe, equalled by his skill in the ring. Presumably, as he aged – he was twenty years past his heyday – he found it easier to subdue opponents by wrestling than by straight knock-outs. On the evening stroll along the Cours Mirabeau, whose plane trees cut a diagonal through the heart of Aix, we suddenly saw the vast figure of Carnera seated at a café table outside the Hôtel Nègre Coste. Flanked by two sinister little chaps who formed his *caudrilla*, Carnera stared at nothing with a catatonic detachment. He had clearly lost any power of reacting to his fellow humans. I wrote in my diary that the Man Mountain appeared to me to be a cross between the writer Julian Maclaren Ross and the film actor Victor Maclagen, a curiously Celtic combination.

Against a background of the Montagne Ste Victoire we had a homage to Cézanne picnic with Tristram, before turning northwards. It was sad to leave Tristram and the Midi, even though we were driving back into spring. Apple trees that had been in bud on our outward passage were now in blossom, the orchards bordered by drifts of acacia and dog roses.

On our way through the province of Berry, we met with a sign *Visitez le Château de George Sand à Nohant*, an irresistible invitation. Up to date my diary had been a stark record of mileage, meals and hotels, but at Nohant I expanded under the influence of a romantic past:

> June 4th. (The only Fourth of June between 1953 and 1963 when we were not at Eton.) . . . [The Château] stands behind gates off a village green, with a church and a tiny *épicerie*. Inside, the house has just been turned into a *musée* by Madame Aurore Sand (Geo. Sand's granddaughter) aged ninety-two and, judging by her picture in early life, a real corker. The furniture was pretty and the wallpapers, particularly the blue ones in salon and bedroom, were enchanting. Maurice Sand (Geo's son) was a painter, who did not quite get going. Graveyard very full.

To this brief note I added a plan of the dinner-table, on whose chairs place cards had been laid to give an idea of the society George Sand had entertained. The table was circular and, clockwise, the diners were, George Sand, Prince Jerome Bonaparte, Gustave Flaubert, Turgenev, Pauline Viardot (for whom George Sand had a passion), Maurice Sand, son of the hostess, and la petite Aurore, seated on a stool between her father and grandmother. French children used to be famous for a sophistication gained from sitting up for dinner in the evening, but even allowing for the literary plums having been selected at one gathering, la petite Aurore must have had a conversational digestif. Undeterred by her ninety years, Madame Aurore Sand had put up a notice in the hall inviting literary visitors to make themselves known to her, but at an early hour of the morning it did not seem wise to take up this invitation.

The graveyard was crowded, but the garden of the chateau, both formal and untidy, was also full of ghosts whose feet had crunched the gravel paths. It was here that Henry James and Edith Wharton had strolled, after admiring the superb collection of marionettes belonging to the theatre of George Sand's children. James had made a careful study of the family tombs in the graveyard, but in the garden he pondered more earthly matters. To quote from Leon Edel's *Henry James: the Master*, 'James surveyed the plain house which had harboured so much ancient passion "And in which of these rooms, I wonder, did George herself sleep? . . . Though in which, indeed, in which indeed, my dear, did she not?"'

After this enthralling visit to the house where, to quote James again, 'they pigged it so thrillingly together', we were halted by meeting a funeral procession. I happened to be driving, so I pulled to the side of the road as the hearse, drawn by a pair of horses as black as pitch, black plumes nodding on their heads, advanced towards us. As I have said, the light Cambridge-blue of our motor car was a novelty in provincial France. Even the closest mourners, walking immediately behind the hearse, cast glances out of their tear-filled eyes, but when the imposing procession was reduced to stragglers interest in this new foreign model was unabated by any attempt to preserve solemnity. Sad as the occasion undoubtedly was, we could at least feel that we had offered a moment's distraction.

Spending the last few days of the tour at Cabourg, we were able to look only at the outside of the Grand Hotel's aquarian dining-room, but Proust's Albertine and her little band could easily be imagined scuttling over the breakwaters of the sea front. When we had left home on 20 May there had been a bus strike in progress. On returning on 10 June, not only was there still a bus strike, but a dock strike had added its own confusion. In France, on the other hand de Gaulle, enigmatically poised on 20 May, was now firmly in the saddle. Our whole trip had covered 1913 miles, while hotels and meals added up to a not unreasonable £141.

XII
A Prophecy Fulfilled

Until I married I had stayed frequently with my grandmother at 18 Montagu Square, which lies parallel to Bryanston Square, where I had been born. The visitors' bedroom looked out over the square and a lack of net curtains allowed opposite neighbours a clear view of one's dressing in the morning. The same lack of protection was a feature of the bathroom at the back of the house, leaving bathers visible to the back rooms of Gloucester Place. This bathroom was regarded by my grandmother's staff of maids as primarily their territory. They made no concessions to visitors, boiling kettles, and washing hair and clothes as the need arose. These activities left a faint but persistent smell of gas, mingling with the reek of the Monkey Brand Powder with which the white tiles that covered the walls were scoured.

Early in 1958 I happened to have called for a friend, Kitty Muggeridge, at her brother's house in Harley Street, Doctor Dobbs being a practitioner who lived over the shop. Drawing a humble parallel with Proust's madeleine, when in the bathroom high up in this tall house I got a whiff of gas and Monkey Brand, the aroma brought back the bathroom of 18 Montagu Square to my memory. No longer were the tall houses of my childhood inhabited by any one family and I felt a strong desire to write of the life that had been lived in them before the high tide of time blotted out the memory. Taking 'The Tall Houses' as a title, I sold this reminiscence to *Queen* magazine, but having begun on this tour of the past I realised that I was squandering material and that a book was struggling to be born. The career prophesied by the girl in Albany Street was beginning to take a more solid form.

Some years earlier we had stayed at Stratfield Saye with my third cousin, Gerald Seventh Duke of Wellington, when Jane Austen had been discussed in passing. In 1958 we were again invited in order to attend the AGM of the Jane Austen Society at Chawton. This was partly the result of my having correctly answered Gerry's two test questions. Where, in Jane Austen is there a scene of transvestism and where is the word 'dung' mentioned? The transvestite scene occurs in *Pride and Prejudice* when one of the officers who so excite the younger Miss Bennets is dressed up in a gown belonging to their vulgar aunt, Mrs Phillips. It is in *Persuasion* that collision with a dung cart is averted by the skill of Mrs Croft's intervention, when out driving with her husband, the genial Admiral.

Gerry, as I have said, had succeeded to the dukedom when his nephew had been killed in Italy, and no inheritor could have taken more pleasure in his position and at the same time worked harder at its responsibilities. My father's great-aunt, Kitty Pakenham, had married the First Duke of Wellington, a union that brought little happiness to either of them, but which did lead to the founding of a dynasty.

Gerry Wellington felt, with some reason, that after the Great Duke, he was the first of his line to rise above mediocrity. He was, however, fond of mentioning that the Second Duke, who died without issue, happened to do so in the waiting-room at Brighton Station, on the way to visit a mistress. His Duchess had been Mistress of the Robes to Queen Victoria, but her husband appears to have found this an unsatisfactory position for a wife.

A tradition grew that a house party from Stratfield Saye should drive over to the Annual General Meeting of the Jane Austen Society, whose membership increased year by year. The meeting was held at Chawton House and in the village the Society had rescued Jane Austen's last home, from whence illness drove her to Winchester and death. An eccentricity of this literary house party was that the two novelists, Anthony Powell and L. P. Hartley, regarded Jane Austen with sincere respect, but with less than total commitment, and jibbed at the esoteric exchanges so enjoyed by Gerry and myself.

Gerry was fond of beginning a story 'In all the years I've stayed in country houses . . .' and I feel the same about the charades acted at Somerhill in July 1958, when John had just left Sandroyd. Mary Soames (née Churchill) was called up to represent Maria Callas, which she did with a bravura worthy of her father's, Sir Winston's, wartime speeches. Anthony Hornby, famous as the most percipient art collector on the Stock Exchange, played the part of a splendidly unctuous clergyman, but the triumph was the acting of *Nautilus*, the American submarine which had recently sailed under the North Pole ice-cap. For 'naughty' a little guest from Thailand called Isra was led in on all fours, with a lead attached to a collar round her neck. She was then reproved when she naughtily lifted her leg against a sofa. 'Louse' was easily conveyed by vigorous scratching and the whole word came together when Anthony, his dinner-jacket buttoned to his chin, came on as the tight-lipped commander of the USN *Nautilus*.

It was in the month of August that Anthony went to the conference in Venice which was to sow the seed of *Temporary Kings*, penultimate volume of *A Dance to the Music of Time*. Soon afterwards, John and I left for a tour of Scotland, starting with a visit to the Glenconners at Glen, before going on north to stay with Antonia and Hugh Fraser on the infinitely romantic island of Eilean Aigus in the Beauly river.

Stephen Spender, also staying at Glen, had recently translated Schiller's *Mary Stuart* and this was to be produced as a feature of the Edinburgh Festival. With grotesque inappropriateness the production was staged in the John Knox Hall, outside of which John Knox himself glowers hugely from a pedestal. As the play includes a scene in which one of Queen Mary's supporters is allowed to visit her in prison and, having been secretly ordained, is able to give her Holy Communion by the Roman Rite, Knox had a stronger reason than usual for glowering.

Henry and Dig Yorke, parents of the Glenconners' then son-in-law Sebastian, were also staying at Glen. When the expedition to the first performance of *Mary Stuart* in Edinburgh was in process of being arranged, Henry's participation presented a problem. He cultivated an intermittent deafness and was thought to be somewhat allergic to theatrical performances. An unsuccessful campaign was launched to leave Henry out of the party going to see *Mary Stuart*, but he became suspicious and a checkmated the plot by borrowing the script from Spender, its translator.

The action of the play took place under strong arc lights in a sort of boxing ring built up in the middle of the John Knox Hall. The actress playing Mary Stuart must have sweated under the double epaulettes of red fox fur which decorated her costume. Suitably for his *nom de plume* of Henry Green, the novelist's face grew even greener. There appeared to be no bar on the premises and it was notorious that Henry required frequent alcoholic stimulus. As Alick Dru remarked of another acquaintance, 'He only did a few miles to the gallon on a very expensive essence.'

As we came out of the John Knox Hall it seemed likely that the motor cars going back to Glen would take some time to appear from a distant car-park. Before I could intervene, Henry Yorke said to John, aged twelve, 'Johnny boy, just run down and see if that's the sign of a pub across the road' and John obligingly skimmed across what seemed to me to be the main traffic artery between John O'Groats and Land's End. Mercifully, the cars drove up just as John had signalled that it was indeed the sign of a pub, so he was recalled. By then, however, my rage had overcome all good manners, and I bawled into the ear of my husband's oldest school friend, 'Henry, if that boy is run over Tony will come and thrash you within an inch of your life.'

Glen had still certain relics of the days when Tennants and Asquiths with their spouses had pursued high ideals of conversation. Elizabeth's super-excellent taste had humanised the ground floor, while leaving the bedrooms as they had been decorated in an earlier period. Christopher told me that the beautiful Paula Gellibrand took extreme umbrage at being given a bedroom whose label on the door seemed to her to read 'Pink Jellies Room'. In fact, the curlicues of Christopher's mother's handwriting concealed the legend 'Pink Trellis Room'.

This Lady Glenconner had been famous for her delicately precious approach to life in general and her family in particular. More practical, Elizabeth her daughter-in-law had installed a ping-pong table in the room where most of the house's life bubbled, which had the advantage of keeping a house party occupied if not exactly quiet. A nearby piano was played in a kind of counterpoint by talented guests. Outside in the garden, below the perron, standard rose trees stood with their feet encircled by violas of the most heavenly blue.

The sun had shone for days at Glen, but the weather broke when John and I set off for Inverness from the Waverley Station in Edinburgh. The weather, in fact, broke so badly that crossing the Forth Bridge the Firth of Forth was invisible. Being unfamiliar with the Highland Line it took me time to realise that the train was going at a walking pace, the storm having brought down the power lines. We arrived at Inverness and Fraserland at an inexcusably late hour, but the Frasers, Hugh and Antonia, were very forgiving.

In the morning there was the nicest of all experiences, that of waking up to a new place arrived at in darkness. Eilean Aigus on its island was hardly in need of additional touches of the picturesque, but early in the last century two brothers lived there under the name of Sobieski Stuart, having convinced themselves that they were the lawful issue of Bonnie Prince Charlie. The drawing-room had doors of double width so that the pair could *faire circle* side by side.

The neighbourhood accepted their pretensions with a polite pinch of salt.

Catching the night train back to London, my niece Rachel, a younger sister of Antonia's, joined us for the long journey south. During dinner we watched with interest a granddaughter of Queen Victoria firmly in control of a situation to which she had certainly not been brought up. This was Princess Alice, Countess of Athlone, then in her middle seventies. When young she must have travelled to and from Scotland in a Royal train, but now she was mucking in with the rest of the passengers in the dining car, absorbed in conversation with a total stranger.

It was Princess Alice who struck a valiant but unavailing blow on television at a legend forever attached to Queen Victoria. Before a nationwide audience of viewers the Princess declared that she had herself asked her grandmother, 'Did you ever say "We are not amused"? "No," said Queen Victoria, "I would never have used such an expression".' But it would be doubtful that if the Queen herself rose from the dead and denied the story on TV she could shake the general desire to believe in such a Royal fatuity.

When roughly a year had passed with Bernard Hollowood in the editor's chair at *Punch*, he wrote to Anthony to say he was abolishing the post of Literary Editor. If by this divorce the editor hoped to rid himself of both the Powells, he must have been disappointed. Freddie Young (B. A. Young), who now distributed books for review, loyally continued to send them to me on a wide front. This belief in my ability to deal with such opposites as a *Life of Lord Haldane*, Secretary of State for War in 1914, and *Italian*

Bouquet, a work that dealt with geography as well as La Cugina, was exceedingly gratifying.

Shortly after this staff reduction on the part of Bernard Hollowood, Jock Murray gave a particularly riotous party in his office at John Murray, surrounded by the relics of Byron. With a crocodile of guests behind him Jock led us down Piccadilly to dinner at Bentley's. Tony insisted that he was among those slightly intoxicated on this occasion, but it was certainly not for that reason that the late John Raymond was kind enough to take me back to wherever I was staying. I did, however, get a shock some ten days later when I met John Raymond at the christening of a great-niece and saw that he had some scabby scars down the side of his face. I could not believe that I had had cause to inflict these injuries, and it was a relief to learn that they were the result of missing a step when mounting an omnibus.

One of the consequences of Anthony's severance from *Punch* was that he no longer spent the first two nights of the week in London as a routine. This pattern had fitted well with the meetings of the Frome District Council, but I think that I had subconsciously been looking for an excuse to resign. The book that was brewing inside me needed the time spent on the council business, when the boredom could only be mitigated by drawing on the agenda. I seized the excuse that my husband had no longer a settled working week to resign.

Our current Rector was a retired civil servant who, after a career begun at the Treasury, had been awarded a CB and had taken Holy Orders. It seemed to me that it would be a pity to waste so much experience of public service, so I promoted his election in my place. Later, I found it wise to keep quiet about the machinations which had led to my replacement if not by a cat among pigeons, then by someone who was not always eager to pour oil on the troubled waters of local affairs.

Originally, when invited to stand for the Frome RDC, I thought that I might make contacts useful when crises arose. This judgement was to be vindicated and not only on the public front. There is a note in my engagement diary for 1958, 'See Mr Manley, 7 p.m.', which was the prelude to a wonderful advance in the management of The Chantry. At the RDC I had learnt that Mr and Mrs Manley were finding their present quarters in the village too cramped for themselves, and their growing son and daughter. As Mr Manley was a preacher and, with Mrs Manley, ran the small but elegant Wesleyan Chapel in Chantry, they did not wish to move. By good fortune the family who had lived in the lodge at our gates had found accommodation elsewhere. My date to see Mr Manley was to offer him the lodge in return for mowing the lawn and guarding the house in our absence. For twenty-three years this arrangement worked admirably. We, our sons and our dynasty of cats loved the Manleys dearly. Additionally, at a Public Inquiry into a proposal to quarry gritstone Mr Manley's evidence obviously impressed the inspector, who decided against what would have been a desecration.

By the end of 1958 I had managed to write 6000 words of what was to be the first of ten or eleven books. The material that I had been squandering on stray articles had begun to coalesce into a consecutive narrative in which the accidents of childhood and the rigours of education came out as a reasonably cheerful story. The prophetess of Albany Street had passed out of my life, but I hope she had further triumphs of clairvoyance.

XIII
The Dance Quickens Its Pace

When we arrived at Chantry two volumes only of *A Dance to the Music of Time* had appeared, *A Question of Upbringing* and *A Buyer's Market.* These had been followed in 1955 by *The Acceptance World*, the upheaval of moving possibly accounting for a longer gap than that between previous volumes. *At Lady Molly's* followed after only a two-year interval, but there would be about three years before *Casanova's Chinese Restaurant* appeared in 1960. This book was finished in 1959, a year filled with a tumult of events.

When André Gide composed the satire *Paludes* (translated as *Marshlands*) he closed arguments and brushed aside disappointments by simply stating that he did not mind boredom, emptiness, monotony, because he was writing *Paludes*. This feeling may sometimes have protected Anthony Powell during the writing of *Dance*, but 1959 was not to be a year remarkable for the emotions against which he had need to build the barriers adumbrated by Gide.

Elizabeth, wife of my brother Frank Pakenham, who had been sent to the House of Lords by Mr Attlee in 1945, gave me a large diary for Christmas. This settled me into a habit of keeping a journal which I have never since abandoned. I cannot pretend that the style of the entries is sparkling, but I do believe them to have been reasonably truthful. Beginning with the holidays of January 1959, when we were lucky to have Mrs Dodd as our holiday cook.

In the post-war years at 1 Chester Gate we suffered from employing a number of females of different nationalities and many varieties of temperament. Then, one December, Providence sent us Mrs Dodd. At her own suggestion she continued to come to Chantry during the school holidays. She was a wonderfully good cook, and became so much part of our lives that she passed on considerable expertise to Tristram and John.

It seems from my diary that the Christmas holidays were a medley of village life and short trips to London. I gave a whoop of joy when I finally resigned from the RDC, and another when Anthony read the first 6000 words of what was to be *Five Out of Six* and found it 'funny'. I had had rather a fancy for *All Those 'I's and 'Me's* as a title, but was convinced by Anthony that this would be impracticable for a customer to ask for in a bookshop. This quotation, from Stendhal's *Vie de Henri Brulard*, remained as an epigraph, but had perhaps lost its relevance.

The installation of the Manley family in the Lodge stabilised our domestic arrangements, but the Stables were still inhabited by a couple whose marriage was becoming ever more precarious. The wife took to sitting on the Coronation seat outside the front gate, dressed practically in evening dress, from where a lorry driver lover would pick her up. The unhappy pair finally left us and each other, and the Stables were gradually reclaimed to house a sequence of tenants, beginning with General Sir Brian Horrocks and his wife Nancy, until, made over to Tristram and John, the house was transformed by them into a spacious dwelling with a magical garden.

The first family gathering of the year was at the wedding of my cousin Richard Rhys, only son of Charles, Lord Dynevor, to Lucy Rothenstein at Westminster Cathedral, Richard having joined the Catholic Church. In spite of the presence of the Cardinal Archbishop, the choir and, indeed, the whole cathedral, it appeared empty and draughty. A lighter note was struck by a beautiful girl, Suna Portman, who was carrying her domestic shopping, a string bag full of carrots and onions.

The bride's father, Sir John Rothenstein, had been Director of the Tate Gallery and that was where the wedding reception was held. Greeted by a waiter with a tray of glasses and the words 'White wine, madam? Champagne with the toasts', a standard was set which led me to escape sickness by a whisker later in the night. With deplorable untidiness I discarded a piece of wedding cake on the toe of Maillol's Venus but at a subsequent Tate party mice seemed to have eaten this nuptial offering to the goddess of love. Two telegrams of congratulation were read out, the first from the President of the United States (Eisenhower) the second from His Holiness the Pope, and there was some question as to the correctness of putting State before Church.

After seven years we had begun to tackle the top floor of The Chantry, where Tristram had appropriated one attic for himself, but the other two rooms were becoming ever increasingly dumps for unwanted furniture and copies of

Autocar. This was in the great days of Stirling Moss, a close friend and associate of our neighbours Rob and Betty Walker at Nunney Court. Their son Robbie was John's constant companion, both at home and travelling to and from Eton. The boys' enthusiasm for a track round which cars could be raced dictated that the new bathroom should be installed in the attic with the best view, but the lesser floor space. These discussions with the builder took place on a frosty day when John fetched the newspapers on foot from Mells Post Office and returned with hoar frost in his hair.

Francis Cruso, the tutor (housemaster) of Tristram and John at Eton, was much loved by all the family, though he was in rather a neurotic state when he paid us a visit in January. This took the form of giving a somewhat *ému* rendering, almost in plain chant, of 'We are now come to take you' from John Betjeman's verses on the 'Arrest of Oscar Wilde'. Francis had recently stayed with the Gladstone family, whose after-dinner entertainment involved listening to Beethoven quartets, while all hands worked on making a carpet. Our offering of billiards, or rather 'slosh', accompanied by glasses of port, seemed enormously frivolous by comparison.

At the end of the holidays John and I went on a day trip to London. As we took in a visit to the dentist, the film *The Great Dictator* and an exhibition at Christie's of the 'Ageless Diamond', grass did not grow under our feet. I had seen the Charlie Chaplin film eighteen years before in Belfast, when it had a certain cachet, as neutralism in the USA had prevented its showing there. I had thought then, and continued to think, that Jack Oakie as Mussolini was funnier than Chaplin as Hitler. He romped through his role, without the lurking feeling of high seriousness that Chaplin brought to his interpretation of the German dictator.

By appealing to the Chairman, Peter Chance, an old friend, we jumped the queue at Christie's for the Ageless Diamond exhibition and, inevitably, saw two near neighbours glaring at us from the slow-moving file. I called the show of diamonds 'delicious', particularly a glittering string described as a 'négligé' for throwing negligently over the shoulders.

It was actually in this month that I handed in my resignation from the Frome Rural District Council of which I have written earlier. Captain Crees, the then chairman, expressed his regrets. They would have been even more powerful had he known how much trouble he was to have from my replacement.

The diary which I kept in 1959 tended to be limited to personal matters, but in February I noted that a man called Hume had been arrested in Switzerland for a murderous bank raid. The news recalled an episode of the early 1950s, briefly mentioned by Anthony in *Faces in My Time*. At that date we were still living in Chester Gate, not far from the second-hand car mart which clogged Warren Street, a thoroughfare parallel to the Euston Road. Motor cars were still hard to come by, and the market flourished in spite of an unsalubrious reputation. One of the dealers, owner of a conspicuous white automobile, was in the habit of parking outside our front door, while bargaining with a prospective buyer. The dealer, of Middle Eastern appearance with a square head and a mauvish complexion, became such a familiar figure that as I staggered home with my shopping basket he acknowledged me with a nod, finally moving on to a faint smile.

Suddenly, Albany Street was agog, when the evening papers came out with the story that the white car of someone called Setty had been abandoned near Regent's Park. Sure enough, there it was in the mews that ran beside our house, and a famous forensic scientist from Scotland Yard was hard at work spraying it for fingerprints. Hardly had this excitement died down when, in the Chester Arms across the road from our house, we found the plain-clothes squad from Albany Street police station obviously celebrating a coup. To the best of my recollection, a wildfowler on the marshes off the Essex coast had come upon some human remains wrapped in pieces of carpet. The head was never found, but it was proved that Hume had cut up Setty's body and dropped the pieces from an aeroplane. It could not be proved, however, that he had actually killed Setty. Consequently, nine years later, Hume was free to attack some unfortunate in Switzerland.

As we continued to be plagued by strangers parking outside our house, I rather callously suggested that a notice reading 'Prolonged search has so far only recovered the torso of the last person who habitually parked here' might act as a deterrent.

This is not quite the end of the story. A year or so after Setty's murder I was recovering from an operation in University College Hospital and happened to be discussing the adjacent Warren Street car mart with one of the nurses. I mentioned that the notorious Setty (he was of Iraqi origin) had parked outside our house. This particular nurse trumped my ace by telling me that she had looked after

Setty when he had been a patient in UCH. 'What', I asked, with some trepidation, 'was the matter with him?'

'He didn't like the shape of his nose,' was the unexpected answer. 'He said it didn't fit comfortably under the yachting cap of the sailing club to which he belonged.'

It was difficult not to speculate that Setty's disapproval of his Creator's handiwork had brought its own retribution.

As a child Anthony bought *Lt-Colonel Seccombe's Army and Navy Birthday Book for Children* with an picture for every day and month. The daily illustrations were small line drawings, sometimes coloured by the owner, accompanied by a verse of varying merit. The monthly pictures were chosen on a different principle: coloured representations of children dressed as soldiers, frequently of the Life Guards, or sailors conducting a battle at the time of Nelson. The film *Bugsy Malone* was made on rather the same principle.

The book was kept by Anthony as a child with the names of his parents and little friends. Then his attention lapsed and was not revived until after our marriage, since when it has been steadily filled in for sixty years. The book makes fascinating reading, not only for the juxtaposition of names, but for the verses allotted by the author. For example, a lady whose romances were notoriously tangled had a verse only too appropriate, 'I've drilled the men wrong, Here's the colonel in sight, They're all muddled up, And I can't get them right.' Many countries and a number of continents are represented, such as the Allies with whom Anthony was in liaison during World War Two, Poles, Czechs, Belgians and French. From the USA James Thurber drew a dear little dog, Chinese and Japanese visitors wrote in their ancient scripts and V. S. Naipaul might be said to have played both for Trinidad and India.

Juxtaposition at times could verge on the surreal. Rosa Lewis of the Cavendish Hotel, famous for louche goings-on by the upper reaches of high society, shared a birthday with Eileen Orwell, wife of George, whose life lay along very different lines. My own birthday, 13 March, a watery date under Pisces, is thickly populated. Besides at least two acquaintances not entered, Elizabeth Glenconner, William Lancaster, son of Osbert and Karen, Betka Zamoyska, daughter of a grand Polish family, Derek Drescher, for long the producer of *Desert Island Discs* for its originator Roy Plumley and, last but far from least, Tessa Davies, a next-door neighbour at Whatley, were all born on this day.

Friday the thirteenth is apt to be called a doubly unlucky date, but in 1959 superstition was flouted and a jolly time was had by at least three of the birthday celebrants at William Lancaster's twenty-first birthday party. I was forty-seven, Elizabeth, who gave the dinner party, forty-five and, of course, William was twenty-one. I danced with Osbert, although our heights were somewhat incompatible. I danced the charleston with David Cecil, an impressionistic folk memory as far as I was concerned. I had an even more energetic *passade* with George Malcolm Thomson, an old steady from the Beaverbrook stable, who had a determination to dance in a pattern of his own. This we did 'till the gunpowder ran out of the heels of our boots'. 'We had a lot of champagne. Home about three,' said my diary.

A week later we drove to Somerhill, where Harry and Rosie Goldsmid were entertaining Antony and Lily Hornby, Madame Marie Edmée Escada, described by Rosie as Lord Beaverbrook's 'French governess', Duncan Sandys, then Minister of Defence, Marie-Claire Hudson, estranged from Lord Hudson, and the Italian Ambassador. His Excellency's rather muted presence was partly explained by the fact that his former chef was now installed at Somerhill. The food was certainly delicious, the implication being that the chef was putting his best foot forward for his previous employer. Anyway, the Ambassador was sent back to London with a parcel of good things, and the chef's compliments.

On Sunday there was something of the atmosphere of a later Henry James novel. Duncan Sandys could be seen walking with Marie-Claire and taking her back to London, presumably in his ministerial car. It was hardly a surprise when they married three years later. The more acute drama involved a smouldering row between Madame Escada and Lily Hornby. Lily, Hungarian by nationality and a ballet dancer by profession, had been rescued from Vienna by Lord Beaverbrook's intervention, shortly before World War Two. Lily had, in turn, escaped from Beaverbrook's circus to marry Antony Hornby, whose taste in pictures was only equalled by his skill on the Stock Exchange. A fellow stockbroker had once asked Antony to pick out a picture, not trusting his own judgement. Meeting this friend as they entered the Stock Exchange Antony said, 'I think I have found a picture for you.' Whereupon another stockbroker, famous as an artistic nullity, said, 'If he doesn't want it I do,' on the principle that one should snap up anything recommended by Antony.

On Sunday evening in the gallery at Somerhill, said to be the longest room in Kent, most of the party split up into couples. Duncan Sandys, over a game of bezique, discussed her plans for the future with Lady Hudson. Rosie, ever a kind hostess, did her best to entertain the melancholy Madame Escada. I played piquet with Antony Hornby, steadily losing, mostly from my inferior play, but also from the distraction of Lily's account of her Beaverbrook life, which she was detailing to Tony just within earshot. I noted that, rather like Casanova's four-hour account of his escape from The Leads, a Venetian prison, this took three hours in the telling.

The Henry James atmosphere continued at dinner with the arrival of Christopher Soames, Mary Soames being the daughter of Sir Winston Churchill, while her elder sister Diana was the separated wife of Duncan Sandys. It was difficult not to be reminded of the possibly apocryphal story that their father, when summing up Il Duce's end, had remarked that Mussolini had at least had the satisfaction of ordering the execution of his son-in-law.

On my way from Somerhill I called at the flat at Bletchingley where, after the death of her husband, my aunt Markie, Lady Dynevor, had come to rest. Cruelly afflicted with arthritis, she put a brave face not only on her illness but on her restricted outlook. Referring to her past life in a romantic Welsh castle she remarked, 'Anyway, I have had it.' It was, to quote the Bible, a treasure no man could take from her.

After being for long out of print, Max Beerbohm's *Seven Men* had recently been reissued. Having given it to Aunt Markie for Christmas, I was able to read to her, not the wonderful 'Enoch Soames', but the terrible story of 'Maltby and Braxton', writers competing to get into grand society. Maltby manages to sabotage an invitation to a high-powered house party which would have brought Braxton into open competition with himself. Throughout the visit the ghost of Braxton appears, visible only to Maltby, causing the wretched Maltby to behave with disastrous ineptitude. I chose to read this story because one of the guests in the house party was Mr A. J. Balfour, frequently entertained by my aunt's mother at Osterley Park and so familiar to her. After her years of kindness to me I can only hope that the reading supplied a few moments of entertainment. A week later the news came that my aunt's struggle was over. Though thankful for her sake, I felt the loss almost as that of a mother.

XIV
Roman Holiday

Besides absorbing what was to be the background of *Temporary Kings* during the conference in Venice, Anthony had made friends with Maria Luisa Astaldi, the art-loving wife of a genial tycoon. Ever hospitable, Maria Luisa, editor of *Ulysse*, welcomed our suggestion of a visit to Rome in May. 'Count on me,' she wrote and was better than her word.

After starting in the Hotel Eliseo, the restrictions of the British travel allowance drove us to abandon this albergo, with its splendid view from the restaurant of floodlit St Peter's, for the Ludovisi, run down but *simpatico*. A fellow guest was Compton Mackenzie, escorted by a younger female friend, with whom he contentedly watched television in the hotel front hall. About ten years later we visited Rome with a tour and found that the *simpatico* Ludovisi had run itself into the ground.

Maria Luisa not only gave a party for Anthony and a German writer (who failed to surface), but sent a car to fetch us to her house. This contained a fine collection of contemporary Italian painting: Morandi, Chirico, Marino

Marini, Kutuzo. The food was very good and so was the literary company. Among the crowd were Mario Prazo (usually referred to as MP for reasons not unconnected with the *mal'occhi*), Ignazio Silone and his Irish wife Darina, and Alberto Moravia, whose novels had been appearing in the UK, together with those of his wife Elsa Morante.

I cannot now remember how, in talking to Moravia, the subject of the relations of parents with their children came to the surface. But I do recall that he told me of a recent experience his wife had had at the hairdresser. One customer had told the hairdresser, 'You must make me as beautiful as possible. My son comes home tomorrow and I know he will want to make love to me.' Shortly after this interesting light on Roman manners, which might have been an incident from the film *La Dolce Vita* then in production, Moravia asked if I would like a lift home. Rather primly, I asked if his wife would be ready to leave. 'She has her own car,' he replied. Even more primly, I said that I thought my husband would be quite ready to go home. With good grace, Moravia drove us back to our hotel. We gave him a drink, but I recorded that he was 'very melancholy'.

Maria Luisa's hospitality continued and blossomed into other gatherings. I feel I should mention that we did make some return by entertaining her to a dinner party at the Travellers Club when she came to London. Kingsley Amis, then married to his first wife Hilly, was among the guests. Kingsley was at the top of his form and kissed Maria Luisa when the time came to say goodbye, an embrace which she accepted in the spirit it was offered.

We knew Alan and Lucy Moorehead from their friendship with the Osbert Lancasters and they were now living in Rome, where, as it happened, they had been married some twenty years before. They had walked up the steps of the Campidoglio before the ceremony, where they had been given a marriage licence that had space for twelve children. Alan had gone to Asola to work on a book, but throughout our visit Lucy was the kindest and most helpful of guides. Of the three children who filled spaces in the marriage certificate, John Moorehead was away in England, but Caroline and Richard were at school in Rome. The latter was of an age to attend the sort of school whose uniform – blue overall, white collar, large bow – was something of an outrage to the son of an Australian father and an English mother.

The British Minister to the Vatican was, as it happened, Marcus Cheke, a friend of Anthony's from Oxford days and known by me as a débutante. Marcus led us to the roof of the colonnade of St Peter's to watch the reception of the bones of Pope Pius X and St John Bosco being received into the Basilica. Pope John XXIII conducted the ceremony, I had last seen him in the Piazza at Venice three years earlier. The dusk fell. Lights flickered, then the flood lighting came on illuminating the façade of St Peter's and the papal guards. As the hearses clip-clopped away the Pope's voice, soft and velvety, implored the prayers of Pius and John Bosco, '*Ora pro nobis*'. Descending in the lift we became mixed up with a river of cardinals, of the deepest rose red.

At Maria Luisa's party we had met Signora Cacciatore, the custodian of the Keats–Shelley house at the bottom of the Spanish Steps. It was February when Keats died there, asking how long this posthumous life was to go on, and there would have been flowers on the steps even so early. 'This morn of Rome and May' the steps were glowing, freesias, violets, lilies and roses just coming into flower. Signora Cacciatore showed us the room that had seen the end of Keats's journey. She had in her hand the draft of the letter that Joseph Severn had begun on a piece of paper where there was already a sketch of a male nude. As she read the last words 'I thought he slept' there were tears in her voice. However deep his appreciation of Keats, in that house Shelley would also seem to be an interloper.

Later that day we changed our tune with tea in the palazzo where MP had his apartment. Everything in it was Empire, including a bidet. Personally I enjoyed his book about this apartment which he called *The House of Life* but other reviewers thought it the dullest of works. Although he had a rather sinister reputation as the author of *The Romantic Agony*, I have wondered if lack of humour was not MP's trouble. He told us, with some outrage, that when T. S. Eliot was asked if there was any Italian poet he wished to meet Eliot replied Ugo Foscolo (died 1827). Apparently this joke was not taken in good part. Escaping from the heavy atmosphere surrounding our host, we had a delicious dinner in the Piazza Navona, but something evil upset me and I was sick throughout the night.

Virginia Bath had urged us to contact her aunt Iris Ledebur, who had settled in the Trastevere. We found her apartment, where she was living with a large black Alsatian dog. When *La Dolce Vita* reached London the following year I disturbed the audience at the Curzon Cinema by squeaking 'I know that dog' at a scene when Iris lay on a couch in a white robe and the Alsatian lay in black contrast beside her. Besides the black Alsatian, Lyndall Birch was living in Iris's flat. This was a daughter of Tom Hopkinson and our old acquaintance, the novelist Antonia White. She had been the fourth, or possibly fifth wife of Lionel 'Bobby' Birch. As we had met him and his sixth and latest wife just before we left for Rome, we began to think this was a count-down of Mrs Birches.

The evening ended with a puppet show in the Palazzo Caetani. This huge house in the via delle Botteghe Oscure (Street of the Dark Shops) had been described by an earlier Princess Caetani and Duchess of Sermoneta as never free from ladders and buckets of whitewash. By now it had been turned into a warren of apartments. The hosts of the puppet show were also entertaining Art Buchwald, famous New Yorker humourist. I heard afterwards that he was depressed because his wife had insisted on bringing their poodle, a frequent runaway, to Rome. Buchwald had objected to having to buy a crate to carry this animal to the Eternal City. When told that he could always sell the crate on arrival, Mr Buchwald remarked sourly, 'Rome, centre of the used-crate market.' A day or two later I saw what was obviously the runaway Buchwald poodle wandering alone on the lawns of the hotels in the via Veneto. His master had been right to feel depressed.

The next morning the walls were plastered with appeals to the citizens of Rome to behave nicely to the King and Queen of Greece, who had arrived on a state visit. The Romans' immediate reaction was to declare a two-hour bus strike. This rendered useless the Roman bus timetable, which had, up to then, enabled us to travel with confidence. We did, however, get picked up by an English woman, who kindly showed us the out-of-town strike-breaking buses.

The timetable itself I brought back to England and gave to Tristram. He was then starting on his first Long Vacation tour, beginning at Rome. Quoting the words with which a Bible is presented to the Sovereign at the Coronation, I told Tristram, 'This is the most precious gift the world affords. Here is wisdom. This is the royal law. These are the lively oracles of God.' And so I believe he found them to be.

It would be wrong to give the impression that we did not follow the sightseeing circuit and devoted ourselves solely to social life. For example, on a day when Marcus Cheke had asked us to luncheon at the British Legation I noted that we went in the morning, first of all, to S. Maria sopra Minerva and then to S. Agostino, where the venerated image of the Virgin Mary wore a high Victoria collar and the Holy Child was wrapped in a golden nappy.

The situation of the Legation, a pleasant house, was spoilt by the eruption of high-rise buildings, planned with no attempt to soften the area with greenery. When we arrived Sir Marcus, the Minister, was addressing a delegation of World Federalists, which included Lord Attlee, the former Prime Minister, and his wife and Clement Davies, a Liberal ex-MP. Waving a bottle of gin in one hand, Marcus explained that it was too early to know what the attitude of the new Pope John XXIII would be towards World Federalism. The delegation looked as if they would prefer drinks to be poured out and that the Pope's goodwill be taken on trust.

I found it possible to chat with Lord Attlee by telling him that I was a sister of Frank Pakenham whom, he said, he was glad to have sent to the House of Lords. I also remembered that he had had a brother killed at Gallipoli, as was my father, and had been on a cruise ship that had visited the cemeteries in 1926, where my mother and my sister Mary were fellow passengers. From there we moved on to Attlee's early days, cycling round as a school inspector, when he was detected to be a socialist because he wore a soft collar. Lord Attlee left me with the impression that he had not had an opportunity to tell such stories for many a long day.

Marcus was to fall ill and die *en poste* only thirteen months later, but during that time he became friends with Pope John XXIII. Lees Mayall told me that when the British Minister to the Holy See was known to be terminally ill, the Pope came to see him and spoke these comforting words: 'Sir Marcus, *vous êtes dans l'état le plus heureux pour un chrétien, vous allez recontrer votre Dieu vis-à-vis. A ce moment je n'ai pour vous que l'envie et l'amour.*'

Although it must have been a temptation, Constance Cheke did not choose that her husband should be buried in the New (1825) Protestant cemetery next to the Old cemetery where Keats lies and of which Shelley wrote, 'It might make one in love with death to think that one should be buried in so sweet a place.' The ashes of Shelley himself were placed in a niche of the Aurelian Wall, which is a boundary of the graveyard. It happened that the day after the Chekes' luncheon party we did visit the cemetery and I found a small flower to put on Keats's grave.

Lucy Moorehead had not only helped me with shopping, but had taken us for a drive to Castel Gandolfo and Lake Albano, where we hoped we had identified the spot at which Stendhal sat and wrote the names of his mistresses in the dust. She now drove us out to a gathering of the friends of Paddy Leigh Fermor in his rented castle. His invitation included a suggestion of staying the night, with a hint that it might be advisable to bring blankets.

Paddy's castle was perched on a wooded knoll, not far from Tivoli. Below were clustered barns and stables, inhabited by a variety of nationalities, flotsam washed up by the tides of war. There was not much in the way of a roof and the furniture was limited to the odd deck-chair, but on the wall of the big hall there was stretched a splendid banner of the Fermor arms. This, Paddy, explained, had been stitched by nuns. 'They looked wonderful bending over it in their coifs,' he said. Two of our party were actually brave enough to spend the night in Paddy's castle, reporting that it was an enjoyable experience, even though the artichoke bed served as a lavatory.

After a visit to the sad little palazzo where the last of the Stuarts, Prince Charles Edward, referred to by my niece Antonia as BPC, and Henry Cardinal of York were born and died, we went on to a party given by the Silones. The host was determined to talk only French, and I heard my genders getting wilder and wilder. Afterwards a party of literati, mostly Irish, dined together at Nino's, where Moravia was seen giving dinner to someone who was not Elsa Morante, but of equally formidable appearance. At the next table the film-producer brother of Pontecorvo, the scientist who defected to Russia, was dining and obviously making a rather fragile blonde.

During the evening we made friends with Denis Devlin and his wife – she, I think, French. He was a poet and Irish ambassador to the Republic of Italy. The following morning they picked us up in the embassy car with the object of going to luncheon at Ninfa, the estate of the Caetanis, Dukes of Sermoneta. The embassy chauffeur had driven for Fangio, World Champion in 1957. This information was conveyed by English spelling, as had the chauffeur himself heard the name 'Fangio' pronounced it was feared that he would display racing technique. As it happened, these skills threatened to be of use, since we had first to drop the Devlins' daughter and her nanny at Ostia. On the way there we passed the derelict site of what was to have been the arena for the Olympic Games in 1940.

Standing forlornly was a circular building, windows gaping, said to have had a purpose known only to Mussolini, of whom no one had had the prescience to enquire. Anthony had developed a crashing cold, so we paused to give him a Fernet Branca, a remedy principally for a hangover. The poor ambassador then got into a panic as to what was obviously going to be a late arrival. He had good reason as, after driving across the campagna and by way of Albano, the dread word Napoli came up on the signposts.

Ninfa lies at the foot of the Apennines, a vast garden in a ruined village brooded over by the remains of a Sermoneta castle. In those days it had a feeling of being like nowhere else in the world, yellow roses growing up tall cypress trees, and among the ruins of seven frescoed churches there ran a small canal, along which arum lilies sailed 'like swans asleep'. Don Ruffredo, the head of the family, was a godson of Liszt, whom he distinctly resembled. He was not very clear as to who was who, but his wife, Princess Marguerite Caetani, was immensely on the spot. She was, by birth, a Boston intellectual and had continued through family tragedies to be editor–promoter of the periodical *Botteghe Oscure*, called after the street where, as already mentioned, the Palazzo Caetani stands.

The day was made more enjoyable by the company of the Devlins. Denis Devlin confided that he sometimes worried as to how he would cope with his seven sisters when his father died. He was obviously an excellent diplomatic representative of his country. It was therefore a sad shock when, at Kingsbridge Station, Dublin, I read that he himself had died, only three months after our visit to Ninfa.

Sean O'Faolain had turned up more than once at various parties and on one of our last evenings arranged for us to meet him for a drink at Ranieri, bringing with him Niccolo Tucci, a contributor to the *New Yorker*. Tucci's half-Russian birth perhaps accounted for the practical joke he played on the *New Yorker* editorial staff, notorious for the heavy-handed editing of contributions. Bored by this governessy attitude, he had typed out 'The Overcoat' by Nikolai Gogol, signing it Nicholas Tucci from the *New Yorker*. He was routinely asked to make a few improvements and enjoyed pointing out that there was indeed one mistake in the surname signed.

Our last party in Rome was once more in the Palazzo Caetani, this time with the head of the British Council. The guests were mostly political and I again found myself struggling with 'the bear from the Abruzzi', Ignazio Silone. I made a note that what he really enjoyed talking about was sex and snobbery, though how I dealt with either in French I cannot imagine.

On getting back to London, I happened to meet Osbert Sitwell in Heywood Hill's bookshop. As a coda to our Roman holiday he told me a story of an occasion when the last, and little, King of Italy was forced to attend a lecture given by the wife of the American ambassador. She lectured on Picasso in Italian, with an inadequate grasp of the nuances, so she was trapped into uttering unconscious obscenities. The King was so delighted that it was difficult to convince him that all lectures were not so lewdly entertaining.

XV
'Jolly Boating Weather'

When Cyril Connolly described the horrors of returning from a holiday, he listed among them 'flight of loved one and success of industrious stay-at-home friends'. On returning from Rome the only immediate horror was the wrong rubber flooring having been laid in a new bathroom. Cyril would probably regard that as an easy let-off.

Immediately, Alan and Jennifer Ross arrived for a night with their son Jonathan, a six-year-old of charming appearance with a golden-brown complexion. At this period we were being tormented by a noxious rubber dump in the ancient Asham Wood, which periodically burst into flames and belched evil-smelling smoke. This it did at five o'clock in the morning of the Rosses' visit. In a rage, I rang up the District Surveyor at breakfast time, but I was pacified by the sight of Jonathan Ross in his pyjamas coming down the attic stairs. He held our Burmese cat, Kingsplay Flixey Fum, in his arms, and was crooning to him in ecstasy.

*

This was John's first Fourth of June and, though William Lancaster had long since left Eton, Karen and Osbert were still kind enough to have us to stay at Henley. There was distinct glamour in the fact that Toby Tennant, of Cruso's, John's house, was Captain of Boats. In celebration the Glenconners, his parents, joined with friends in hiring a boat that was moored very prettily at a timber yard below Windsor Bridge. Before we joined the party for dinner we watched the up-river procession of boats. It is the duty of the coxes, dressed as eighteenth-century admirals, to call out to the crew in numbers so that the boat's balance is steady when they rise to their feet. On this occasion one of *Hibernia*'s oars overbalanced and the boat swamped.

After dinner in the gathering dusk, the Captain of Boats party marched down Eton High Street and on to the edge of the Thames. The castle was illuminated without being fiercely floodlit, and the fire works began with rockets, at which it was traditional for the audience to count the bursts, sometimes as many as six. The climax was a set piece against which the procession of boats came down-stream, the oarsmen once more rising to their feet. This was when *Hibernia* swamped yet again. Toby Tennant, Captain of Boats, was not best pleased, however much the onlookers relished the drama. His mother remarked that he was looking 'pretty grim'. However, the wet bob responsible for this double disaster survived to become a well-known voice on Radio 4 on Sunday morning. Tris-tram, Ferdie Mount and Henry Harrod, who had shared our luncheon picnic, returned to their respective Oxford Colleges, into which they successfully climbed.

This was the first summer when Arthur and Rosemary Mizener came to stay. Arthur Mizener taught English Literature at Cornell, up-state New York. His book on

Scott Fitzgerald, *The Far Side of Paradise*, first of what was to become an industry, had made a considerable impact, drawing attention to a writer who, incredible as it may now seem, was tottering on the edge of oblivion. When the magazine *Esquire* brought out a number pin-pointing the whereabouts of important literary figures Arthur stood out alone at Cornell like a lighthouse in an undistinguished ocean. This was before Alison Lurie had blossomed, also at Cornell, into a respected and formidable novelist and teacher of English.

The furniture in the visitors' bedrooms was still on the scanty side. To remedy this I took two Empire armchairs superfluous to our needs to Bradford-on-Avon, where two friends had a three-storey antique business. For four pounds and the two chairs we acquired a chest of drawers, but the enjoyable part of the transaction was prowling round the premises, where there were relics to be found of one of the partners' earlier career on the stage. He had played Bingley in the production of *Pride and Prejudice* where Celia Johnson had made a great success as Elizabeth Bennet. The other partner was slightly afflicted with a stutter, but this did not prevent him from discussing sexual symbolism in the stars, a tongue twister if ever there was one.

This rearrangement of furniture was designed to make the Mizeners more comfortable. They arrived in a new motor car, a Jaguar, which they were going to take out to astonish Cornell. We allowed them to drive this new toy, sold to Arthur as 'ricing green' in colour, to a number of local parties. At home we entertained a literary neighbour, barely met previously. He brought with him a friend, perhaps a secretary. The latter made Rosemary Mizener the interesting confidence that his parents could not possibly have joined the party as they would not have known how to behave. A week later, our literary neighbour happened to be at Westbury Station, when he was kind enough to say that he had found our dinner party 'a most civilised occasion'. This was how someone in *Tender Is the Night* described a party of Dick Diver's. Perhaps the influence of Arthur had brought out the Scott Fitzgerald phraseology.

Although a tradition had grown up of a house party at Stratfield Saye for the AGM of the Jane Austen Society to which we were annually invited, we had not, in 1959, found the simplest approach. This was a well-known puzzle, and Gerry's eldest brother had done his best for his guests by compiling a route in which they were urged to turn round and go back for one mile. That was the approach from Reading. It was several years before I worked out that the problem of coming from the west could be solved by skirting Basingstoke and arriving at the gates of the park. This route eluded Leslie Hartley, who directed his succession of eccentric drivers along a labyrinth of lanes, possibly pausing at any convenient public house for directions.

Anthony had always maintained that the First Duke of Wellington (Gerry preferred the adjective 'First' to 'Great') had chosen Stratfield Saye as a gift from a grateful nation because the park had contours which recalled a battlefield. In this park stands the parish church, built in the form of a Greek Orthodox basilica. On our first visit Gerry pointed out that his nephew, the Sixth Duke killed in Italy in 1943, to whom Gerry had succeeded, was what he called 'very democratic'. This had taken the form of abolishing the gallery which had been the family pew, leaving a rather meaningless empty space. I shall have given a poor idea of Gerry's character if anyone is surprised to read that he managed, in a few years, to restore the gallery in which, as he said, the First Duke had worshipped.

On this July Sunday afternoon I walked round the battlefield park with Leslie. I found him very wrought-up, discussing the complications which attended his visits to Italy. He even admitted, with a touch of shamefaced pride, that he had been accused of having *mal'occhi*. It was the custom at Stratfield Saye to play Scrabble after dinner, a pastime deplored by Anthony, but enjoyed by me. Leslie was so jumpy that he found it difficult to grapple with the game's intricacies. Gerry, on the other hand, chased the will o' the wisp of the top score word 'jonquils'.

Stratfield Saye had not been the home of Gerry's childhood and the histories of past neglect served to highlight his remarkable rescue job, adding such individual effects as carpets in the drawing-room especially woven in a Spanish factory. This was particularly appropriate, because the pictures in this room had been captured in the baggage train of Napoleon's brother Joseph, when retreating before Wellington's advance and the King of Spain, restored to his throne, had declared that Wellington had the right to keep them. Gerry's delight in his inheritance was, of course, combined with expertise. James Lees-Milne, a great friend, has described how, in 1943, he helped to unpack ormolu wall-brackets, ordered from Paris by the First Duke and remaining in their boxes for about a century, until they were at last appreciated.

*

A recent excitement in Chantry Village might have appealed to Gerry, who enjoyed stories of outrageous sexual behaviour. The cowman from Manor Farm, whose conversations with his cows as he brought them in to be milked were enjoyed by the neighbourhood, called unexpectedly on the Secretary of the Women's Institute. Brandishing a handful of pound notes, he demanded that she, in her eighties, should go to bed with him. Not unduly discomposed, she refused the money and a sympathetic police patrol removed the septuagenarian suitor until his ardour had cooled. The secretary was broadminded on such matters. She once spoke to me almost with contempt of a niece who objected to her husband's straying. 'When my husband was away in South America, if he hadn't taken up with somebody I should have thought he needed new tickets.'

From this rather Hardyesque situation, we went to London to attend a party at the Tate Galley, by which the Friends of the Tate hoped to encourage supporters. It was a hot night and tempers were not at their easiest. Ian Fleming was fulminating that the only solution to life's problems was a divorce, but that this was hideously expensive. Later, at Ann Fleming's invitation, Debo Devonshire drove Ann, Anthony and me back to the Flemings' house in Victoria Square for a drink. The peace of the evening was suddenly wrecked by the crash of the front door and the voice of the creator of James Bond as he came storming up the stairs. It had taken on that high-pitched note which I remembered from the hunting field of someone cursing at being cut in on. This peahen scream endorsed Somerville and Ross's theory that half those who go out hunting do so in a state of blue funk. Ian Fleming was hardly in a blue funk, but he obviously expected to find his wife entertaining guests of whom he had a right to complain. A beautiful duchess and a married couple who were little more than acquaintances hardly provided the material for the sort of row that Ian had come home with the intention of making. A week later Ann gave a supper party at which Ian threw his arm round me and made a public apology.

On the Wiltshire–Somerset borders there was a big rally for a wedding at Tisbury. Anthony was rather incensed that I had told various friends that he would not be wearing a morning coat. As it happened he had Henry Bath, Michael Pitt-Rivers, Isaiah Berlin and Christopher Sykes to keep him in countenance in ordinary plain clothes. Christopher Sykes added an extra dash with a grey bowler (white, I think, in hatter's language). This was the hat which had aroused the envy and emulation of Evelyn Waugh. Christopher and I shared a famous cousin in Admiral Sir William Pakenham and enjoyed discussing his faultless turn-out. We agreed that no one knew the meaning of whiteness who had not seen the white slip which Cousin Willie habitually wore edging his waistcoat.

It was also a matter for discussion with Christopher as to how much truth there was in Claude Farrère's novel *La Bataille*, where a British naval officer resembling Willie Pakenham was blackmailed by the Japanese Admiral, whose wife he had seduced, to direct operations at the battle of Tsushima.

At the return home after this wedding, pleasure was somewhat dissipated by the discovery that a pretty lead urn had been stolen from a plinth in the front drive. Anthony's great-grandfather, Thomas Robert Jefferson, heavily carved in marble, was cemented in place of the urn, his weight having, so far, proved a deterrent to robbers.

Glad as I was, in general, to have left Chester Gate, I did miss the enjoyment of the Open Air Theatre which brought Shakespeare to our doorstep. It was therefore a pleasure in this July of 1959 to set off for Old Wardour Castle, where the Stowe Historians had come down from Northamptonshire to perform *Richard II*. Even the rain could not detract from the charm of the setting and the splendid melancholy of the play, which begins with King Richard's arbitrary exiling of his cousin Bolingbroke and ends with Bolingbroke, now crowned as Henry IV, contemplating the corpse of 'the mightiest of his greatest enemies, Richard of Bordeaux'. There is much wit in the flowing lines, but little cheerfulness. The producer of the Stowe Historians, however, enlivened the last act by introducing a knockabout element into the scene in which the Duke of York, uncle of both Richard and Henry, discovers that his son, Aumerle, is in a plot to assassinate Henry. Keen to be on the winning side, York tells a servant to bring his boots, in order to lay his son's treason before the reigning monarch. The Duchess, a mother hen, strives to prevent her husband from getting his boots and urges Aumerle to take advantage of the delay to grab his father's horse and get to the King first. She herself will follow at once. The boy who played the Duchess made a great success as an angry ageing woman setting off at a gallop to extort a pardon for her errant son.

The rain had stopped half-way through the performance, but it was enjoyable to find supper and hot drinks in what I remember as a sort of Gothic pavilion, or garden house. The school holidays had begun and neighbours crowded round. Among them was Sonia Orwell, then married to Michael Pitt-Rivers, whose home was King John's House,

Tollard Royal. Sonia was interested to find that King John was a hero to the Tollard Royal schoolchildren. She said that they cried when they discovered that he rated as the wickedest of English kings. Sonia was herself somewhat shaky on English kings and their succession, asking me if Richard II was the son of Edward the Confessor.

After this enjoyable outing Anthony assured me that I looked positively rejuvenated.

XVI
The Long Haul to Felbrigg

In the backwash from the Suez débâcle it was still difficult, if not impossible, to get a visa to visit Egypt from the Egyptian embassy in London. Tristram, setting out on this first Long Vacation tour, did not mention his idea that he might proceed from Rome to Egypt via Athens. Luckily, his reassuring postcard that he had got back from Egypt arrived before the one telling us that he was going there, on a visa issued in Rome, but would be 'very careful'. He brought back with him a photograph of himself with a charming Greek family in L'Aiglon, an Alexandrian night-club, having made friends with a young man, Christoliero Nimakis, on the boat from Athens. After this adventure Tristram said that he felt he had reached home when, at Venice, he recognised the blonde barge man who had ferried us to the Regatta Storica in 1956.

Tristram's return was awaited with eagerness, as we were at the point of leaving for our semi-annual visit to Wyndham Ketton-Cremer at Felbrigg Hall, his magnificent house inland from Cromer. These had started in the first summer of our married life, when we had made what we called Mr and Mrs Sponge's Sporting Tour. We found that money was running short while at the Scole Inn, Diss. Anthony telephoned Wyndham Ketton-Cremer, whom he had known at Oxford. I had never met Wyndham before, but it seemed in no time at all that he had become Tristram's godfather and a host to all four Powells.

It was a long haul from Chantry to Felbrigg. This year, 1959, was one of those when we broke the journey by staying with Pam and Michael Berry (later Hartwell) at Oving. I had known Oving in the past, when I had taken my brother Frank's horse Baalam out hunting from the Berry family's farm outside Aylesbury. The nearest blacksmith had been at Oving, and we used to take the horses to be shod by way of field paths and green lanes. The Berrys' house had the same view as that from the forge, with the icing sugar towers of Waddesdon Park shining across the Vale of Aylesbury.

There was a terrace which took full advantage of this view, and on one of our visits we dined out there with Pam and Michael. Pam kindly asked me if I was feeling cold and I replied I was not, because I was wearing a suspender belt. This reminded Michael of an incident in his Eton career. 'I was walking down Eton High Street,' he recalled, 'when a boy walking behind me said to his companion, "Berry has quite a good figure." "Yes," said the friend, "you know he wears stays."' Anthony and I agreed that this was an almost perfect Etonian anecdote.

Wyndham Ketton-Cremer has told the story of Felbrigg in a book written with scholarship and love. Round the earlier part of the building the balustrade reads 'Gloria Deo in Excelsis' in letters of stone. For many of the former owners of Felbrigg this might have been a rather equivocal legend to surmount their home, but for Wyndham, a faithful Anglican, it had a certain appropriateness. His dedication to the church did not, however, preclude him from recounting stories of the vagaries of the Norfolk clergy, which ranged from the eccentric to the spectacular. This latter was the occasion when Wyndham had the enjoyment of seeing a magistrate from the local Bench administering a colossal kick on the bottom of the delinquent Rector of Stiffkey. The magistrate had to resign from the Bench, but the Rector of Stiffkey was finally demolished by a lion in a cage on the front at Blackpool.

In his history of Felbrigg, Wyndham described how his father watched unprotesting in polite impotence as his uncle allowed the house and estate to fall ever more into decay, while money was raised by the unnecessary sale of books and china. The house and contents had been bought intact in 1860, causing some local derision at the acquisition of the inherited possessions of the Wyndham family by a businessman unrelated to the ancient family of Wyndham. This broken continuity was restored by Wyndham's grandfather, who married a wife descended from an authentic line of that family.

By the time we came to frequent Felbrigg it had been brought into excellent order, though the strain may have shortened Wyndham's father's life. The long period of decay was also responsible for the preservation of the house very much as it had been in the mid-nineteenth century. There was no electricity until after World War Two and this held off requisitioning, which caused such havoc in neighbouring estates. Indoors, the visitors' lavatory depended on a tenuous linkage of pipes. Wyndham's first important book was a study of Horace Walpole. He had in consequence made friends with the great collector of Walpoliana, W. S. 'Lefty' Lewis and his wife, who came to visit Felbrigg. The Lewises, most courteous of New Englanders, were so appalled at this example of East Anglian plumbing that they were unable to conceal their feelings. Agreeing that the pipes leaked and froze, Wyndham eventually installed a less Heath Robinson model.

The grander parts of the house were still intact, including the collection of English and Dutch pictures. Of the latter, a sea battle between Chinese junks and Dutch battleships had the possibly unique spectacle of the Chinese Admiral conducting operations on horseback from the shore. To me the most magical room in the house was the dining-room: white stucco decorations, blue-washed walls and portraits obligingly dressed to match their surroundings. Wyndham was endearingly keen on food and appreciated his guests' enjoyment.

Mrs Ketton-Cremer, towards whom Wyndham had a devotion verging on the fussy, after rescuing Felbrigg from dereliction had withdrawn to a small house of her own in the neighbouring parish of Metton. As one of her son's friends said, she was happiest when surrounded by wool and kittens. That was indoors. Out of doors, Mrs Ketton-Cremer had a weakness for collecting donkeys, which a neighbouring farmer turned to his profit by setting ill-kempt animals to graze in a field across the stream that bordered this kindly woman's garden. The farmer astutely gauged how much the market would stand, and the donkeys bought and nursed back to fitness by Wyndham's mother and his brother Dick were undeniably picturesque.

Neither Dick, who died in the Battle of Crete, nor his mother were remotely on Wyndham's intellectual level, but he was determined to appear unpatronising.

Besides ourselves, a frequent visitor at Felbrigg was the historian John Bowle. He had been an Oxford friend of Wyndham's, having earlier been at Marlborough with John Betjeman. The latter always referred to Bowle as John Edward, which it was difficult to avoid doing to his face. Between Betjeman and Bowle there was a deep-seated enmity based on the days when, as struggling young men, Bowle had ousted Betjeman as secretary to Sir Horace Plunkett, the much mistrusted uncle of my aunt Beatrice's husband Dunsany.

John Edward was known as a brilliant teacher of history, both at Eton and at Westminster. It was only too easy to address him as Chips, from the film *Goodbye Mr Chips*, a 1939 success. Playing *bouts rimés*, Wyndham created the opening line, 'Come, Muse, and sing the praise of Mr Chips', which was followed by 'He eats the passion fruit and spits the pips'. It was not quite clear if John Edward was more flattered or affronted. At one time he was engaged on a book that I thought he should call *All About Everything*, of which I can only remember one quotation: 'At this date the birth of Jesus Christ may be supposed to have taken place, an event from which the world has not yet recovered.' Bowle then thought that this was going rather far for a master at schools where Christianity was the official religion, and replaced the words with 'since when the world has never been the same'.

To the sorrow of a host of friends and many godchildren (one of the penalties of bachelorhood) Wyndham died in 1969. His mother had died about ten years after the loss of his brother Dick, which had left Felbrigg without an heir, but with the work of preservation practically completed. Wyndham had linked many of his projects to occasions of national rejoicings, replanting a woodland so that the rides formed a V for Victory and rebuilding the dove house in the kitchen garden to celebrate the coronation of Queen Elizabeth II. On what I think was our last visit, I drew a picture of Wyndham in coloured chalks, sitting in his favourite chair beside the stove in the great hall. Behind him there hung a small but charming painting of the square tower of Cromer church. My likeness of Wyndham may not have been immediately recognisable, but no one could have mistaken the picture of Cromer church.

The long haul home from Felbrigg could be broken at a number of points, but it was only in the summer of 1959 that the boys and I turned aside from the main Buckingham–Oxford road to explore Juniper Hill, the hamlet that was the scene of Flora Thompson's classic, *Lark Rise to Candleford*. Juniper lay very close to Tusmore Park, which I used to visit when the banker and racehorse owner Vivian Hugh Smith, later Lord Bicester, had bought the former seat of the Howards of Effingham. Under the coat of arms which dominated the magnificent gateway was inscribed the legend 'God save the King and the Howards'. To mark the change of ownership, one of the Vivian Smith sons climbed up with a piece of chalk in his hand in order to write 'And the Smiths', an assertion of equality from what F. E. Smith, Lord Birkenhead, described as 'The greatest family in the world'.

It was a hot afternoon and when we reached the scattered houses of Juniper there was no sign of life, apart from a row of elderly men seated on a bench outside the public house, the Fox. I remembered that in Flora Thompson's day the women of the village knew that the then pub, the Waggon and Horses, would turn out when they heard the last song in the evening's repertoire, 'The Outlandish Knight'. Flora Thompson's own rather alcoholic father was, I think, in the building trade. He would have been a cut above the farm labourers who frequented the local beer house, where the grandfathers of the villagers sitting outside the Fox would have been singing ballads preserved by Flora's literary genius.

Leaving Juniper Hill to its slumbers, we drove on and crossed the Cherwell valley, to arrive at the church of St Mary the Virgin, North Aston. John Piper in *A Shell Guide to Oxfordshire* has described as 'a joke' the closeness of the church to North Aston Hall, only a narrow passageway separating the two buildings. My parents moved into this house shortly before my birth. My brothers and sisters, living in hired houses as my father's military career dictated, may have felt that our Irish home was the pivot of their lives, but to me my mother's insistence on Pakenham Hall being the inheritance of my eldest brother had prevented me from feeling that it was where my roots lay.

North Aston church was as I remembered it from thirty years before, the recumbent tomb of Sir John Anne and his wife dividing the mysteriously dark chancel from the Victorian Lady Chapel, where light poured through unpainted windows. In the porch there still hung a handwritten Roll of Honour of the First World War, my father's name heading a list of seven casualties from this small village. An early lesson in village discord had been given me when a meeting to decide on a more permanent memorial had been unable to agree on the rival merits of stone, wood, alabaster and white marble, this last being the most popular. Stalemate was reached when the chairman declared that anyone who had served in the late war would want to forget all about it.

The church itself stood, as it were, on an island surrounded by the gardens of the Hall and it was never quite clear how many rights of way were open to worshippers. With the boys I climbed the steps by which we had straggled to church for seventeen years. The ground floor of the Hall was improved by a tangle of climbing roses, which added a sleeping beauty quality to a house where french windows were open but no humans were to be seen. I remembered only too well that the drive past the house was certainly private, but I could not resist driving through the forbidden territory. Having been warned to look out for possible objectors, John reported that someone was looking out of a window on the north-west corner of the building.

This room had been the schoolroom, light, airy, but plagued in autumn with flies that the efforts of a tame wren were powerless to subdue. The wren took liberties, flying out of one room to exit by a window in another. Once it even made a mess on the party frock of a cousin spread out on the bed. (The cousin got her own back by giving my sister Julia and me a complaint which combined the symptoms of both varieties of measles, with a touch of scarlet fever.) I did not pause to see who was looking out of the window, in case it should have been myself. Nor was I able to identify which among a group of oak trees was the one grown from an acorn at my birth and planted out by me on my seventh birthday. Indeed, they all seemed equally gnarled.

XVII
The End of an Irish Era

Earlier I have described the redecoration of Pakenham Hall by Edward and Christine, which had taken place in 1925. Thirty-four years later little had been added, though Mrs Cruickshank, the cook-housekeeper of Lucullan gifts had left to look after her brother, a gardener retired from Dunsany Castle. It was five years since I had stayed with Edward and Christine, and when I arrived with John it seemed that I had changed more in that time than had the house in three decades. Its endearing individual smell was, however, still constant: polish, wood smoke, damp, mitigated by the hot-water pipes, installed after the plans of Maria Edgeworth's father, a cousin and a neighbour. A feeling of emptiness that occasional visits from nephews and nieces had been powerless to banish still hung over the nurseries on the top floor.

As things fell out, this was a brief visit, but there was time to make a foray to Lough Deravaragh, when Edward and John were rowed out by the keeper, while Christine and I gossiped on the shore. I wish now that I had induced her to describe the days before she had met Edward, when her friend Flora Grierson had introduced her to Lady Ottoline Morrell's circus at Garsington.

Flora, elegantly beautiful, was the daughter of Sir Herbert Grierson, a literary figure who held the chair of English at the University of Edinburgh. In appearance Christine must have been a complete foil to her friend, for her looks and figure could have been done justice to by Wyndham Lewis. Recollecting Lady Ottoline's portrait by Augustus John, it can even be speculated that Christine looked more in keeping with the circle at Garsington than the conventionally exquisite Flora. At the wedding of Edward and Christine she, alone among the guests, had dressed as for a garden party, in flowing violet-blue chiffon with vivid lipstick and nail varnish to match.

The following morning after visiting the lake – it was my last morning of the old dispensation – Edward and Christine left for Dublin, where their life was really lived among the players of the Longford productions at the Gate Theatre. These were the years I have mentioned, when they only came to Pakenham for the moment when the bluebells covered the woods with a blue flame and for the annual school treats for the Castlepollard schoolchildren. Proportionately, two hundred Catholics came on one day and thirty Protestants on the next. These treats had, I believe, been instituted by my mother on the model of those held at her own childhood home and were originally called, she told me, 'Her ladyship's afternoon parties'.

We could not know that it was to be the last goodbye to Edward as we stood in the porch which had so often been photographed as a background to departures. 'Give my love to Eton,' Edward said. 'Not that anyone would remember me now.' In unison John and I said, 'Alf would' – with perfect truth, for Alf was the long-serving controller of Rafts, who with his phenomenal memory would have had no difficulty in recalling that Edward had rowed in the *Monarch*, the ten-oar boat filled by a mixture of celebrities, which led the procession of boats on the Fourth of June.

It was a wild, wet day and the house felt gloomy after Edward and Christine had left. I remembered a speech from Ivy Compton-Burnett's *A House and Its Head*. 'This house has to be so different from other houses, and lately I have felt it too much for me, all this difference.' The gloom lifted, however, when John and I resorted to the billiard room. There could be found the big round-top brown trunk that I remembered from nursery days, when it led a narrow-squeak of a life of just not being left on the pier at Dun Laoghaire. Besides a letter from the First Duke of Wellington to his sister-in-law Lady Longford, accepting to come to the church for the marriage of her daughter Georgiana, but not to the breakfast, this trunk contained my mother's diaries, from her later girlhood to her death in 1933 at the age of fifty-six.

The letter from Wellington had a more than historical interest for me, because the bride, Lady Georgiana Pakenham, had an only daughter, Georgiana Evans-Freke, who was the kindest of spinster godmothers to me and from whom I had my second name. I was wearing her grandmother's (my great-grandmother's) wedding veil when I was christened Violet Georgiana, and it was draped over both Tristram and John at their baptisms. My mother's diaries were a far more exciting affair. She had left a request that these should be sent from London, where she died, to be kept unopened at Pakenham for fifty years. Somewhat remote from the confidence of her children she may have been, but it is hard to feel that from her knowledge of her descendants she could have supposed that such a wish would be respected.

My mother did not have a gift for narrative, but she had strong feelings, so that her comments on people and their actions cast more light on her own character than on that of her subjects. She had watched with appalled fascination the love affairs of her eldest sister, which evolved into a tangle of fiancés. She knew her mother hoped that she would be proposed to by Lord Beauchamp and she wrote that his home, Madresfield, with its romantic moat, was her favourite house. But it was Lord Beauchamp's cousin, Lord Longford, who, in fact, proposed to her. Considering that Lord Beauchamp subsequently fled the country because of a homosexual scandal, my mother might have been said to have had a lucky escape. When I happened to mention Lord Beauchamp's departure abroad, my mother euphemistically remarked, 'Oh you know he's under a cloud, do you?' This expression could be used to cover financial irregularity as well as sexual deviation. Before I closed the lid on the trunk, which held forty years of my mother's life, I learnt with some relief that she had been pleased at my enjoyment of my first London season, although it was in those summer months that she was told that besides her chronic arthritis she had developed more sinister symptoms.

Not only was this to be the last goodbye to Edward, but it was the last sight of Andrews the butler, who had come to Edward and Christine when they married. Although he was occasionally known to contemplate finding another post, tempted by a long-time girl-friend who had, as it happened, been lady's maid to Katharine Asquith's mother, he stayed on until he suddenly collapsed and died, as it were, in harness. His sniff when the talk took a turn of which he disapproved was notorious and sometimes inhibited the conversation at dinner. Dispensing with a footman did not cause him to give notice, for by that time he had become a powerful local figure in Castlepollard. Robert, the last footman, went on to the then Duke and Duchess of York, and followed them to Buckingham Palace when they became King and Queen. Andrews expressed some disapproval of the domestic arrangements at the Palace, by which the footmen were off one day and on the next. Robert was kind enough to welcome those of the family and other guests he had known at Pakenham when they turned up at Buckingham Palace parties.

A wild storm was raging as we left for Dunsany. In Castlepollard slates from the roof of Hennessey's, the main bar and grocery, were airborne, but Randal's passion for social life was unabated. Our first outing was to dine with the Nesbit Waddingtons at Beaulieu, near Drogheda. Owing to their political attitudes and unwillingness to compromise intellectually with their neighbours, Edward's and Christine's circle had been both eccentric and limited. It was an enormous pleasure to me to be taken to a number of houses to which my brother and his wife had been strangers.

Beaulieu was both the earliest and the most perfect Caroline house in Ireland. Nesbit Waddington, who had married the Montgomery heiress to whom it had descended, had managed the Aga Khan's Irish stud. I had not seen him since débutante days. Also invited to dinner was a figure from my early life, Clementine Beit. At school she had been to my sister Julia and me the most entrancing among the younger girls. She was the posthumous child of Clement Mitford, killed in World War One. Consequently, the father of Nancy and her flock of sisters succeeded as Lord Redesdale. Had Clementine been a boy, as Evelyn Waugh pointed out to Nancy, the latter might have found herself brought up on the strip of land in Canada where her father hoped to strike it lucky.

Clementine had married Sir Alfred Beit and they had restored Russborough, Co. Kildare, where Victorian taste had wrecked the splendid Palladian façade by replacing the glazing bars with plate glass. When the glazing bars had been restored, the magnificent Beit collection of pictures was installed and Russborough returned to its former splendour.

On the way back to Dunsany at two o'clock in the morning the Boyne lay beautiful. The Boyne had meant a great deal to my uncle Dunsany and his fascination with the river gives charm to his earlier books, before his works degenerated into rather meaningless novels. I have written earlier of Dunsany's possible influence on Hemingway. I may add that they were both large men, who relished big-game shooting. They both happened to go on safari in Africa with Philip Percival, the famous white hunter. Dunsany was always suspicious that his ideas might be pinched by other writers, so it is debatable if he would have appreciated having a hand in another's literary revolution.

Oh, gay lapped the waves on the shores of Lough Ennel
And sweet smelt the breeze 'mid the garlic and fennel
But sweeter and gayer than either of these
Were the songs of the birds in Lord Belvedere's trees.

Betjeman's narrative poem 'Sir John Piers' came to mind

when Sheila drove me to tea at Belvedere, which is poised on terraces above the lake. In the poem this is the background for the seduction by Sir John Piers of Lady Cloncurry, wife of the patriot, who was awarded two hundred and twenty thousand pounds damages for crim con. This vast sum ruined Piers, who must have regretted that he had wagered to bring off the seduction. Betjeman describes him as dying in penurious misery in the Isle of Man. The Cloncurrys, on the other hand, both married again, Lady Cloncurry taking as her second husband what must have been a distinctly broadminded clergyman.

Belvedere had descended to Colonel Charles Howard Bury, who had led an expedition up Mount Everest in the 1920s. He did not look as if he would be interested in seducing peeresses, but enlivened our visit with an account of another scandal. The wife of an eighteenth-century Lord Belvedere had confessed to adultery with his brother. He incarcerated her at a house, where she was forbidden to see any society except her servants, until after his death, which was thirty years later. Not content with this unpleasantness, Lord Belvedere quarrelled with another brother and built the largest sham ruin in Ireland to blot out his brother's house. A more agreeable sight than this ruin was the view over Lough Ennel, which on that Sunday afternoon was dotted with boats of varying sizes, in which the inhabitants of the county town of Mullingar were disporting themselves.

Ireland is notorious for the distances that are driven for social events. Beaulieu and Belvedere were a mere twenty miles or so from Dunsany, but a day or two later I was unsuspectingly taken on a far longer jaunt. Sheila wished to stay at home and persuaded me to attend a dinner party with Randal, which was said to be a drive of forty miles. I only realised when starting at six thirty that forty miles did not include the twenty miles to Dublin. The host was a Welsh tycoon, who had built a house overlooking the St George's Channel where Lycidas had drowned. His wife was a beauty and her face had for years appeared on hoardings to advertise one of the most popular brands of cigarettes. I was enthralled by the fact that her looks had been almost exactly described by Anthony in *A Dance to the Music of Time*, in the shape of Mona, married to Peter Templer.

Under a waning moon, we started back on the long drive to Dunsany. I thought it prudent to speak to Randal at intervals of five minutes. In one of these bursts of conversation he told me of an incident in the North African campaign, where he had served with the Guides Cavalry. Detailed to lead an Allied unit in a retreat, he found that the speed of their vehicles was such that he was covering, rather than leading, the operation. I think this may have been the occasion of which a military historian wrote that Randal Plunkett made himself very unpopular with the Planners, when he took his carriers through the Quattera Depression, both sides having considered this to be an impassable obstacle.

As the night wore on I began to recognise landmarks, which I remembered from a few days' hunting near Dunsany. To my horror we turned another way, in order to inspect the combine that was ploughing barley by moonlight. It was two o'clock in the morning and Randal finally yielded to my appeal to go home. The combine was a new toy, to mitigate what one of the farm-hands had remarked of last year's wet ploughing: 'Hardship and slavery'.

That was far from the toughest drive of the Irish Grand Tour. The following day, with Sheila at the wheel of her Mercedes, Beatrice 'Bebe', daughter of Randal and Sheila, John and I set out for Co. Cork. John and Bebe had to be dropped at different friends, while Sheila and I had to make our way to Co. Waterford. Sheila drove across Ireland from Leinster to Munster at a speed that Oliver Cromwell would have envied, touching eighty miles per hour. Pausing at the infinitely impressive cathedral on the Rock of Cashel, I was fascinated by the carving on the tympanum of the north door, where a centaur with his bow at full stretch tramples a dragon beneath his hooves. Sheila remarked that she had just seen, among the crowd of tourists, the owner of a fine collection of pictures. To my surprise I recognised Hugo Pitman, whom I had met as a neighbour of my sister Pansy in Wiltshire, and who was a patron of my artist brother-in-law Henry Lamb, but this was no moment to renew acquaintance with someone known to be afflicted with deafness.

The city of Cork was remarkable for a large and modern cinema built to accommodate a Film Festival and as Ireland was suffering, uncharacteristically, from a drought, it was a relief to find lavatories that flushed. It was here that John and I watched Terry-Thomas in *Carleton Browne of the FO*, a film unworthy of his genius. Meanwhile, Sheila drove on to deposit Bebe at Rosscarbery, on the edge of the Somerville and Ross country. It was from Somerville and Ross that I knew that the women of Munster wore heavy cloaks with hoods lined with a satiny material. It was rather a surprise to see two women so dressed standing outside the principal hotel. To appear thus becloaked in a heatwave must have come from a deep-rooted determination to profit from being picturesque and the stamina to support it.

That infinitely melancholy book *Burke's Country Houses, Volume I: Ireland* describes Castlemary, Cloyne, as a ruin burnt in the 1920s, though the family had converted the stable buildings into a dwelling house. This was the next stopping place, the mother of John's Sandroyd friends, the Galitzine brothers, being then married to the owner. The former stable yard had been planted with palms and rhododendrons, among which the boys weaved at speed on their bicycles. They were still inhabitants of what Charlotte M. Yonge called 'the Alsatia of boyhood'.

This Celtic marathon then led us across country over which I had followed the United Hunt thirty years before. My ignorance of hunting had been profound and by jumping too close to a tree I had struck off the pommel of a borrowed side-saddle. Finally we arrived for the night at Cappoquin, one of the smaller mansions that, with Dromana and Lismore Castle, dominate the River Blackwater. This was the home of Sir Richard Keane and his wife Olivia. A portrait by Maurice Grieffenhagen of the previous baronet, Sir John, presided over his descendant, who described his father's slightly unusual career. 'Like a cook, he had to have a day off in each week.'

Like the cloaked peasant women of Munster, Sheila's stamina was undefeated. She drove us back to Dublin, then on to Dunsany, where we played a set of tennis at which I could hardly hit a ball. In my diary I wrote that my legs hurt so much that I did not sleep until 2 a.m.

Undeterred, Sheila left with Randal on the following day to stay with Henry Maclehenny in Donegal for a day's stalking. I understand that the deer were sometimes faced with the choice of standing as targets or swimming the Atlantic. Left alone in my glory at Dunsany Castle, I settled down to write in the library, a room not much used in the days of my aunt and uncle, but made very habitable for Sheila and Randal. As I struggled with my book, a small mouse ran along the panelling in front of me, obviously a literary type.

The next day was spent with John's Eton friend Peter Ind, whose large house at Bray, Co. Wicklow, was bursting with three generations of the family. The party included two or three French boys, one of whom, the son of the chef d'équipe of the French jumping team competing at Dublin Horse Show, was of a smoothness seldom seen among Irishmen of his age. A diversion took place when a man called with the possibility of buying a pony from the Inds for his little boy. The deal fell through, but this possible buyer's appearance reminded me of the demeanour of Flurry Knox as described in *Some Experiences of an Irish RM*, 'having in unusual perfection the gravity of manner that is bred by horse dealing'.

The last stage of this Homeric Irish tour was at Killruddery, the home of the Brabazons, Earls of Meath, and a place magnificently laid out, on much the same principle as La Granja near Segovia or, indeed, as Chatsworth. The pattern is of a house facing ornamental water, with a steep hill down which a cascade flows on one hand, while the vista on the other is closed by further hills. This brings Co. Kildare, Old Castille and Derbyshire together, distant in geography, but near in feeling.

Tony Meath's grandfather, who founded a now forgotten festival, Empire Day, had returned from a trip up the Nile with a tent that was lined with Arabic symbols in bright colours. Betty Meath, with whom I had shared an Oxfordshire childhood, was slim with a deceptive air of fragility. She organised a wonderful picnic on the Wicklow Mountains for ten or eleven, of which the centre-piece was this Egyptian tent, transported in a lorry driven by Tony Meath. I was privileged to sit beside him and so had a fine situation from which to look down on Sally Gap and Luggalaa. The following night charades culminated in Laurence Methuen-Campbell, brother-in-law of the host, miming the cutting of someone's throat, dismembering the body and packing it into a suitcase. For me this was to be the last of a particular kind of Irish country house visiting, but it undeniably ended with a flourish.

XVIII
Summer Ending

The dead end of August is a notoriously discouraging period, but the wonderful benefit of leaving London is that of not returning to streets where dried leaves rustle with garbage in the gutters and the parks are burnt brown. Summer's end had still some time to run, in this year of 1959, and I found that the book I was writing was taking shape. As I said earlier I had suggested calling it *All those 'I's and 'Me's*, a quotation from Stendhal on the difficulties of autobiography. Anthony, as I have already mentioned, thought this would be a difficult title to enquire for in a bookshop. I saw his point about the sound of super egoism and settled for *Five Out of Six*, my position in my family. Later my niece Antonia suggested that she might write her life story and call it *One Over the Eight*, which was what she had been born.

On the last day of August the Rector, a civil servant retired before taking Holy Orders of whom I have already written, came to tea. He discussed my religious deficiencies, and moved on to plans for clearing the chancel of Chantry church of choir stalls and advancing the altar, so that the celebrant could officiate facing the congregation. This fashion was said to be all the go in France. It is remarkable that all rectors, High, Low or Broad, have always wanted to pull the church to pieces, regardless of the fact that it is a perfect example of mid-nineteenth-century craftsmanship. The Rector's attitude had long before been celebrated by John Betjeman:

> He did take down the pew ends,
> And sold them anywhere,
> But kindly spared a few ends,
> Worked up into a chair.

Some weeks later at the Harvest Festival, the Rector invited a Franciscan from the Anglican Monastery at Cerne Abbas (home of the well-endowed giant) to preach. The visitor wore a Franciscan habit, brown frock, with the three knots in the girdle for Poverty, Chastity and Obedience. The effect was, however, ruined by the Rector's refusal to sit down and he remained standing immediately behind the preacher. This may have been from a wish to demonstrate that the chancel stalls were unsafe to use and should be removed. It has been reported that the women of Cerne Abbas consider the giant to be a proper figure of a man, but what the Franciscans with their vow of chastity think can only be imagined.

My sister-in-law, Christine, had been brought up in Cheddar before her mother, Amy Trew, moved to Oxford. Mrs Trew's father had been, I believe, the agent of Lord Bath, owner of the Cheddar caves and the Cheddar Gorge. Henry Bath still took a keen interest in promoting this ancient haunt of tourists and the last outing of these summer holidays was a party given by the Baths for what can only be called a Cheddar Gorge Extravaganza.

A troupe of Central European acrobats, the White Devils, had been engaged, with the promise that their star, Rudi, would walk across Cheddar Gorge with no net stretched to break his possible fall. The White Devils were a family company of two generations. While Henry was entertaining his friends on the roof of the Cheddar Restaurant it became clear that there was unusual cause for anxiety. Gradually it was explained that it had been necessary to buy a new rope to cross the Gorge from side to side and that this was far oilier than the ones on which the White Devils were accustomed to practise their art.

After frantic scrubbings with detergent the rope was at last stretched across the Gorge and the blindfolded figure of Rudi, the leading White Devil, began his crossing. His mother (I think she must have been) watched his progress with her hands clasped in prayer. There was a slip, or even two, and Rudi sat down to change his socks at least once. The lone figure with his long balancing pole could well have been an image of the voyage of the soul, including the halt to change socks. There was also the haunting feeling that a fall could not fail to involve casualties among the crowds gazing up from below. I subsequently asked a friend, a county court judge officiating in the neighbourhood, if this danger had been brought to the notice of the authorities. He replied, 'Not till afterwards.'

Apart from her anxiety that her family was out of control and consequent awkwardnesses, my mother had got on well with a wide range of acquaintances on both sides of the Irish Channel. This was before widowhood, and the increasing bad health of which she was ashamed, reduced her social life to occasional forays among her friends. She had, however, one woman friend whose life was a distorted reflection of her own. Olive Baring had been born Olive Smith into the large family of a banker, Hugh Smith. Like my mother, she had had six children and her husband had been killed in action. There was even a distinct physical resemblance between them, but Mrs Baring carried my mother's tendency to muddle her financial affairs to heights which required annual rescue by her brothers, many of whom were successful City operators.

I am writing these details of Olive Baring because I had so recently reread my mother's diaries in which she figured as a girlhood friend. She was brought to tea at Chantry a few days after Rudi had walked across Cheddar Gorge, when she was staying with Henry Bath's sister Lady Kathleen Stanley. One of Olive Baring's sons had recently given her a pug dog, which she had brought with her to Lady Kathleen's pretty Gothic Revival home, a former rectory. Mrs Baring blithely ignored her hostess's seething indignation at the totally unhouse-trained behaviour of 'Pog'. He had been so called because a German prince had, in his owner's youth, remarked, 'The pog he is a seldom dog.'

Mrs Baring was full of questions as to the state of Pakenham. She particularly enquired if the lion and lioness in Dresden porcelain still sat on their red velvet plinths in the front hall. I was able to assure her that these examples of the zoo created for the Japanese Palace of the King of Saxony (at Longleat there are more specimens) were still in place. I did not add that it was unwise to admire any of Edward's inherited possessions, owing to his habit of selling anything thought to be of value in support of his theatrical enterprise, and to make a poor bargain.

That lion and lioness, Olive Baring remarked, had been wedding presents from the Napers of Loughcrew, a neighbouring Palladian house thought to be under a curse which brought about its periodic destruction by fire. The pair of jungle felines struck me as an unusual present from country neighbours and, on consulting my sister Mary, I found that Mrs Baring's lively imagination had been at work. The present from the Napers of Loughcrew had, in fact, been a china pot of vast size and great hideousness. At tea-time, with the Napers present, a chain of thought started in Mrs Baring's mind. 'And what', she had asked my mother, 'did you decide to do with that terrible china pot? You thought of putting it in the housekeeper's room.'

The last days of summer were overshadowed by the prospect of a General Election on 8 October. The neighbour who had taken on the task of chivvying to the polls one hundred electors of Whatley and Chantry provided a horse box as a Conservative Committee Room. Some years later this devoted worker in the Conservative cause nearly resigned from the party, when he realised that public money was being spent on buying the Leonardo cartoon of *The Virgin and Child with St Anne*. In the meantime, however, he rounded up the voters assisted by me, with the guilty knowledge that I was going to sneak off to London to go to the *Daily Telegraph* Election Night party, of which I have written earlier.

Owing to the Conservatives scooping the pool, this 1959 General Election was rather muted as far as the *Daily Telegraph* party was concerned. The next day Pamela Berry gave an end of Election luncheon party in the River Room at the Savoy, which had an intimacy that the party of the night before had lacked. I sat between two friends, Christopher Glenconner and Hugh Trevor-Roper, not yet Lord Dacre. Anthony sat between two beauties, Lady Diana Cooper and Pamela, wife of John Wyndham, the latter not yet Lord Egremont. Practically the last return to come in was the loss by a Liberal of his West Country seat. This was greeted with a burst of applause for a mixture of personal and political reasons. In my diary I made few political comments, but after this Conservative landslide I did make the rather obvious remark that, from then on, then Labour party would be Trade Union run, which for a period turned out to be the case.

Evelyn Waugh's life of *Ronald Knox* appeared in October, and it seemed to me that though Waugh had overestimated Ronald's position as a preacher and theologian, he had managed to subdue many of his own manias. As a preacher Ronald's position was neatly summed up by the Duke of Norfolk, who wrote asking him to give the address at his wedding. 'You know the sort of thing I mean,' wrote the leading Roman Catholic layman. 'Something for which five minutes is too short and ten minutes too long.' This splendid assessment of any sermon might well be followed by clergymen of all denominations. As a note on this I found myself in a congregation of two at an early Celebration at Whatley. Undeterred, the Rector did not abide by the Norfolk rules and preached at length on the theme that adultery (but for women only) used to be punishable by death.

The last expedition before winter set in was the drive to luncheon with the Waughs at Combe Florey, about forty-five miles distant. To those who had known Piers Court, Stinchcombe, it was interesting to see what had fitted in and what had not. The bookshelves of that 'ridiculous library', as someone unkindly called it, were now dwarfed by a room on a larger scale than the one for which they had been designed. On the other hand, the staircase showed off a many-lustred ornament to perfection. Evelyn himself was proud of the carpet he had commissioned the Wilton carpet factory to weave for him, from a design the same factory had made for the Great Exhibition of 1851. He took pleasure in explaining that the makers almost rebelled at the task, protesting that anyone prepared to spend a thousand pounds usually chose something in better taste. Undeniably, it did stab one in the eyes, all the more so because the furniture was scanty.

Evelyn had been pleased by respectful reviews of his *Ronald Knox*, though I made a note that Graham Greene had suggested that Evelyn had painted Ronnie in colours too sober and clean. Graham would perhaps have enjoyed the story current in the village of Mells, that when Monsignor Knox was asked, during a drought, 'Are they short of water at the Manor?' he had replied, 'No idea, haven't touched the stuff for thirty years.' Although there would be more than five years before Evelyn succumbed to an almost suicidal habit of life, on this visit he already appeared to be far from well.

October moved towards its close with a hotting up of the running battle between me and the Rector. To foil his attempts to gut Chantry church I pointed out that the pews of Holy Trinity (1848) were just as vital to the pattern of the church as those of Babington (1742) which I have earlier described, there being barely a hundred years between the two buildings. This so goaded the Rector that he declared that if he were curator of the 'Babington Museum', as he chose to call it, he would tear out the box pews.

I closed the month with a quotation from a poem by James Joyce:

> The last wasp of summer left buzzing alone.
> All her loathsome companions are faded and gone.

XIX
Twenty-five Years On

The month of November began with my reading the typescript of *Casanova's Chinese Restaurant*, which I found to be an infinitely touching memorial to Constant Lambert. Although it was only eight years since Constant collapsed and left an unfillable gap, it did by then seem a very long time since he made one of his most individual telephone calls, which were indeed unlike anyone else's. Once he was suffering from a sore throat and croaked over the wire that he felt like Mimi in *La bohème*: 'Bbetter . . . much bbetter.'

Since the death of Anthony's mother in the spring of 1954 his father had become ever less willing to leave the hotel on Richmond Hill, their settled residence from soon after the end of World War Two. At first he had stayed with us not infrequently, on such anniversaries as my mother-in-law's birthday. Then, as he had confessed to Anthony, he felt like an animal, only secure when near his den. No longer did he give me or the boys luncheon at his club, the Rag (the Army and Navy), where his mood had varied from the hospitable – oysters or, on occasion, a bottle of Burgundy – to excessive gloom.

At the beginning of November I went down to Richmond to see my father-in-law for what turned out to be the last time. During World War Two I had spent more than a year sharing a house at Petersham, two miles from Richmond. Dining in London, it was vital to catch a train to Richmond Station that connected with the last bus out to Petersham. On one occasion I failed to make the connection and I have always insisted that I covered the two miles in twenty minutes, wings being given to my feet by the sinister area of scrub round the bottom of Richmond Hill, fit lurking place for rapists and murderers.

On this November afternoon the view from Richmond Hill was at its most reminiscent of a painting by Richard Wilson, the Thames shining in a golden haze. Colonel Powell was also in a relatively golden mood. He inhabited a big room in which he had a large radiogramophone and a collection of Victor Sylvester *Come Dancing* records. I do not think he particularly liked them, but he had a magpie's instinct for collecting, even including paper bags of graduated size and underclothes stored according to their age.

Owing to his highly nervous temperament, Colonel Powell was only too apt to get on the wrong side of people with whom he dealt in daily life. Residence in hotels offered particular opportunities for rows, which at times even threatened expulsion. On the other hand he could inspire considerable devotion in his everyday contacts and as a young man he was distinctly handsome. When we inherited a number of photographs of him as a subaltern, Eve Disher, whose success as a painter came rather late in her long life, felt really devastated that she had never had the opportunity of meeting the fascinating young Philip Powell. After my visit in November his health became ever more shaky and on the last day of 1959 I travelled to London with the object of persuading him that he must have a brief respite in a nursing home. I was apprehensive of this mission, dictated by his doctor, and could feel that I had escaped from a painful situation when I found that my father-in-law had died before I reached London.

This is, however, looking ahead. In the meantime I found myself in trouble with the Rector and his wife from a verbal misunderstanding. The Rector, it was obvious, had been handing out his savings for church expenses. Unfortunately my remark that this was 'immoral', meaning for the parish to accept the gifts without making an effort to raise funds itself, was taken to mean that I considered the Rector's munificence to be immoral. My tactlessness resulted in the Rector's wife refusing to speak to me for five years, but I still think she went too far in blaming me for her husband's attack of shingles being psychosomatic.

Our silver wedding began to approach with an inevitability that surprised me, though I had, as already described, bought Anthony an Empire bed and he had given me a wonderful drawing. At the original ceremony I had been suffering from a particularly vicious attack of influenza, which I had carried with me across Europe on the Orient Express to Athens. To nurse this condition I had retired early to the top bunk. When the Italian passport officers called, I blurted out through my snuffles, '*Je me suis couchée parce que je suis terriblement enrhumée.*' My newly made husband enquired, 'Why did you say you had gone to bed because it was more roomy?'

Staying with the Lancasters at Henley to take John out from Eton for St Andrew's Day I began to feel that history might repeat itself. Luckily, a bilious attack was not entirely disabling and I was able to collect bunches of ilex leaves from the gardens of Leicester House. With the ilex leaves and strips of silver tinsel the big front room at the Travellers Club was made festive and even prettier by candles in the silver candlesticks of which the club possesses handsome examples.

Before a party there is always an anxious moment, on this occasion smoothed over by the hall porter, who presented us with a silver wedding card in which he had composed a poem with an apt reference to *The Music of Time*. I had wondered who would be the first guest to arrive and it was delightful that it should have been Alick Dru. Until the last instant, when he stepped on to the train at Minehead, he had been a doubtful starter.

Counting what in the hunting field is called 'outliers', a hundred and seventeen people actually turned up and, as obviously there must have been refusals and absentees, we had probably invited fifty more. Presents were all useful and beautiful, from a tiny silver flask to some rose bushes wrapped in silver paper. I believe that there had been complaints from members of the Travellers that the black leather armchairs were a dingy background against which to entertain female guests. On the contrary, nothing could have shown up evening dresses more effectively. At least two people who met there for the first time, Toby Tennant and Emma Cavendish, married and have long since celebrated their own silver wedding. In the course of the evening I asked Anthony's publisher – always called Frere, but actually A. S. Frere, Chairman of Heinemann's – if I might send him the book I had just laboriously finished typing and, in a jocular mood, he agreed that I might do so.

Twenty-five years before, I had made the mistake of collecting the cards attached to our wedding presents without, being in something of a fever, making a list of the donors. On a smaller scale I repeated this mistake, but there was one present which was easily identified. Tristram, up at Trinity, Oxford, had asked the President if he could take a carving from off the chapel which was being replaced by a new model. This Tristram gave us and, cemented on to the front of The Chantry, the angel's head has weathered thirty-five years without disintegrating.

In mid-December we went to dine with Sonia and Michael Pitt-Rivers at King John's house, to meet Cyril Connolly and Deirdre, whom he had recently married. Michael told us that we were eating venison from Cranborne Chase, such as King John might have transfixed with an arrow. I quoted 'the tall tense deer' from an early poem of e. e. cummings, 'all in green my love came riding', which Cyril picked up, emerging from a jumpy mood. Discussing the pattern of the girls he fancied, Cyril had slotted them into the categories of the dark consoler, the redhead and the extreme blonde. This certainly matched the pattern of his wives as far as appearances went, Jeannie, Barbara and Deirdre in that order.

On the day that Anthony finished *Casanova's Chinese Restaurant*, the most elegiac volume of *A Dance to the Music of Time*, I was faced with a problem that had to be solved every December. Having once been established as the President of the Chantry Women's Institute it was my duty to give an address at the last meeting of the year. I would have enjoyed reading the ending of *Casanova's Chinese*

Restaurant, with its ominous picture of the Ghost Railway, but instead I gave the assembled members an extract from Philip Sidney's *Arcadia*, which did not have an unusually soporific effect on the company.

We may have started the month of December by giving a party, but we were far from the only hosts. Arabella and Mark Boxer entertained at the Lotus House, Edgware Road. As I was staying with my sister Mary, I was given a lift home soon after midnight by Osbert Lancaster, while Anthony did not get home till 3 a.m. This rout was followed by the Venetian Blind at the Royal College of Arts. Everyone, men and women, took full advantage of the Longhi style of hats and masks. Osbert, in a cloak and hat borrowed from the Covent Garden wardrobe, made a sinister impression with a mask painted white. Arabella Boxer, on the other hand, in a scarlet tunic and tights could have passed among the crowd in a Carpaccio without any remark.

On Boxing Day we went over to Lady Juliet Duff's house at Wilton, where I quoted to myself Blucher's comment on London: 'What a city to loot.' Her Christmas guests consisted of one bright and cheerful lady, Diana Cooper, and three collapsed gentlemen of a younger generation, Alan Pryce-Jones, Michael Renshaw and Peter Coats. All three lack the stamina of Juliet and Diana, of whom they could easily have been the sons. The year came to an end at Ann Fleming's party, where I found myself singing 'Auld Lang Syne', one hand in that of my brother Frank and the other in that of Lady Violet Bonham-Carter, who I always felt may have suspected me of making a mock of the name we shared.

Just before Christmas I had received a letter from Frere

of Heinemann's. He wrote that he would be prepared to publish *Five Out of Six*, 'though lamentably lacking in sex, scandal or bad taste'. This was both the fulfilment of the prophecy of the blonde girl in the Albany Street wool shop and the Departure Platform for a new career.

Index